An Aliyah Journal

Moving Up

by Laura Ben-David

Mazo Publishers
Jerusalem, Israel

Moving Up

ISBN: 965-7344-14-X

Published by:
Mazo Publishers
Chaim Mazo, Publisher
P.O. Box 36084
Jerusalem 91360 Israel

Website: www.mazopublishers.com
Email: info@mazopublishers.com
USA: 1-815-301-3559
Israel: 054-7294-565

Contact The Author
Laura Ben-David
P.O. Box 193
Neve Daniel, Israel

Email: bendavid.laura@gmail.com
Website: www.aliyahbook.com

Cover Design: Avi Levine

To my family

Table Of Contents

Acknowledgments

Moving Up is not a story about me; it is a chronicle about Aliyah, as seen through my eyes, and written with my pen. The journal is not a work of fiction. Names, characters, places, and incidents are all real and any resemblances to actual persons are hardly coincidental.

Many people have gone in and out of my life, and have given character and flavor to *Moving Up* simply by being themselves. If you think a character in the journal might be you or someone you know, it probably is, and for that, thank you!

After all of the writing that I did to produce a whole book and beyond, I find it immensely difficult to write one page to recognize and thank every individual who made *Moving Up* possible. However, here is my humble attempt.

First, I want to thank my husband, Lawrence, my partner in our Aliyah and in life; you have been with me all the way. To my children, Shira, Lexi, Eitan and Ezra, who were *shlepped* with us, but kept on smiling, and to Yaakov, our Sabra, who will have to read the book himself one day, thank you for being such an important part of this journal.

I would like to express my true gratitude to the following people: Rabbi Yehoshua Fass and Tony Gelbart for not only starting the revolution of North American Aliyah, but for starting it exactly on time for *our* aliyah; Rabbi Kenneth Brander, your strong commitment to Israel influenced us in so many ways; My parents, Marty and Carol Ginsberg, you were the driving force behind the completion of the book, and made it possible; My publisher, Chaim Mazo, you are not only a great publisher, but a fine human being; Avi Levine, for your friendship, patience and talent in making the book cover just right; Mike Stocker, the photojournalist whose much-used photo of me, with my mouth wide open, coming off the plane, has now found a final resting place on the cover of this book; and thanks goes to Mike and the Sun-Sentinel newspaper of South Florida for allowing the use of your photos in this book.

To my brother Steven, for getting me started, and to my sisters Amy,

Hindy, and Hudi, my sister-in-law Becca, and my brothers-in-law Steve, and Adam, for being my sounding board and for helping to proofread the book; To my Uncle Marvin and Aunt Dinah Fishman, and your wonderful family, for your unending support of my journal; to Shelly Sanders and Sylvia Herskowitz for your proofreading expertise and to Jonathan Goldfus and Tani Bayer for your creative contributions. To Sam, Ori, and Steve for making my website happen and for making things happen on my website.

Thank you to everyone else who helped me in so many ways, big and small: Rafi and Atzila Abbo, Laura 'Across-the-Street', Yael Adler, Michael Barnett, Howie and Chanie Bryks, Rabbi Emanuel Feldman, Shaul Goldstein, my Aunt Ilene and Uncle Dick Karson, Daniel and Elana Kaszovitz, Moshe Kurzmann, Devorah Levine, Emily and Barry Lifschitz, Judy Lowy, my Aunt Wittie Lynn, Haim Makovsky, Ariela and Jeffrey Port, Sherry Roseman, Shani Simkovitz, Pinny and Tzippy Sivan, Howie and Judy Warter, Dani Wassner, Sara Weinreb, and I know there are many others and I do apologize to anyone I may have missed.

A special thank you to the wonderful people who believed enough in my book to make it possible through their generous sponsorships; to the Gush Etzion Foundation for their tremendous support; and finally, to all of my loyal readers (many who have been reading my journal entries from the beginning), for your terrific feedback, encouragement, and your genuine thirst for stories from Israel, which has truly powered my writing!

I wish to say, from the bottom of my heart to all, thank you.

Laura

Foreword

by Rabbi Yehoshua Fass

For centuries, Jews throughout the world have yearned, prayed, sung, and studied about returning to *Israel*, and throughout our tumultuous Diaspora experience, that very dream of returning home has sustained our people.

Close to sixty years ago, with the creation of the State of Israel, a dream that seemed so elusive became a reality. What most Jews throughout history were deprived of in their lifetime, could now be a precious reality for a new generation.

While North American Jewry did not pick up *en masse* and immigrate to Israel, a significant number of Americans did – more than 150,000 made the journey home. Whether it is for national, ideological, or spiritual reasons, Americans are continuing to choose to make *Aliyah* because of their deep bond and connection to the land and the Jewish people.

Although one man or woman's move is a fulfillment of a personal journey, its impact is felt and embraced by an entire country. In this small country of Israel, every person counts. Israelis eagerly anticipate the talent, the entrepreneurship, the contributions, the Zionistic ideological passion, and the Western education and professionalism that are embodied in all *Olim* that arrive on Aliyah from North America.

It is with each and every new *Oleh* that Israel is enhanced and continues to prosper. The doctor, the teacher, the actor, the physical therapist, the musician, are all, in their own way, building Israel, one person at a time.

Therefore, when any book, memoir, or publication is published, it is received with excitement and encouragement for it helps stress the viability of living one's dream in Israel and the fulfillment of our national destiny.

We applaud Laura Ben-David for her honest, inspiring, and

humorous *Aliyah* memoirs. The reader will follow her on her emotional roller coaster as she experiences the trials and the triumphs of establishing her family in her new home in Israel. Many will discover a modern Israel that they were unaware of and some might even follow in her footsteps...

Rabbi Yehoshua Fass
Founder & Executive Director
Nefesh B'Nefesh
www.nefeshbnefesh.org
Email: info@nbn.org.il
North America: 1-866-4-ALIYAH
Israel: 02-659-5700

Introduction

More than nine years before my family's *Aliyah,* my husband, Lawrence, and I moved our family from Monsey, New York to Boca Raton, Florida and decided that we would move to Israel two years from then. Needless to say THAT didn't happen. As is often the case, our two-year plan turned into a five-year plan, and finally ceased to be a plan at all; until the most unlikely of times.

In the fall of 2000, the Arabs launched their Intifada on Israel. Suddenly, the number of tour buses in Israel was dropping while the number of bombed buses was rising. And rising. Talk of Aliyah was almost nonexistent as people everywhere were even canceling their trips to Israel.

The Ben-David Family

While all this was happening, a big change took place that brought Israel back into our minds: Everyone was talking about Israel! Besides that it was constantly in the news, nearly every sermon at our synagogue put a huge focus on Israel. One day Lawrence and I looked at each other and wondered whatever had happened to our Aliyah plans. Suddenly, like an old light bulb that got switched on and kept growing brighter and brighter, we just knew that we needed to make Aliyah. Then it was only a matter of a few months until we formulated our plan to move with our four children who then were ages 11, 9, 6 and 4. It was January 2001 – that summer was a bit too soon – so we penciled in the date of Summer 2002. And that is exactly when we went.

Soon after the exciting announcement of our decision, we bumped into friends of ours at a restaurant. They told us how happy they were for us and how they wished that they, too, could make Aliyah.

I tried to encourage them, but they explained that since he is a rabbi it would be very difficult to make a living because rabbis are "a dime a dozen" in Israel. But that is not the end of that story.

Within a few months after that meeting, the rabbi received the tragic news that an Arab terrorist had murdered a young relative of his who was on his way to school. Spurred into action, he changed his destiny – and the destinies of thousands of others. His name is Rabbi Yehoshua Fass and he co-founded *Nefesh B'Nefesh*, (Jewish Souls United). The organization's main goal being to "revitalize North American Aliyah and to expand it for generations to come." Rabbi Fass created the means for his family to move to Israel; and a legacy to enable thousands of others to do the same.

Amazingly enough, their very first planeload of North Americans moving to Israel was scheduled for...Summer 2002! We were going with them!

The first step in our preparation was bringing the children into the planning process. While major life decisions may not be for children to make, we felt it was important for each one of our children to be an integral part of the process and feel positive, if not altogether excited about the move.

Lawrence and I began to slowly introduce various exciting aspects of Israel through stories, photos and books. Our goal was to familiarize our children with Israel while stimulating conversation and dialogue. Additionally, we started to plan our children's first visit to Israel, which would be a vacation for them, while actually being a pilot trip for us.

At this point we had not made any official announcement or decision. While speaking with my second daughter, 9-year-old Lexi, I mentioned that we were thinking of moving out of South Florida, just to see what she thought of the idea. She thought it was great and suggested New York, where we had previously lived, and had much family. I vetoed New York, so she promptly suggested we move to Israel. I told her I thought it was a great idea and we should tell the family.

That was it. I let her announce it to the other kids, and everyone was very excited about the adventure and mystery of moving to a new country, and one that is so dear to our hearts. Well, that wasn't really it. There were many times that Lexi wanted to "take back" her brilliant idea to move to Israel. And her sister and brothers had what to say too.

Shira, our oldest daughter, who was eleven at the time, was a bit excited, but also quite nervous about starting over in a new school, new community, new friends, and new language; very valid concerns, I might add, and ones that we would all have to deal with.

Six-year-old Eitan was probably the least perturbed at the thought of moving, but was apprehensive about leaving the school and friends he had grown very fond of. Being a laid-back kind of kid, he took the news in stride.

Ezra, who was only four, already knew enough to know that he didn't like going anywhere at all. Not to school, not to visit anyone, and certainly not to go someplace 6,000 miles away. Yet young as he was, I was not very worried. After all, eventually wherever he would live would be called "here" and he could just stay there when he didn't want to go anywhere.

As for Lexi, she had some second thoughts as the move drew closer. A grade behind Shira, she watched all of Shira's friends have their bat-mitzvah parties throughout our final year until it dawned on her that she was going to miss nearly all of her own friends' bat-mitzvahs. This very nearly devastated her.

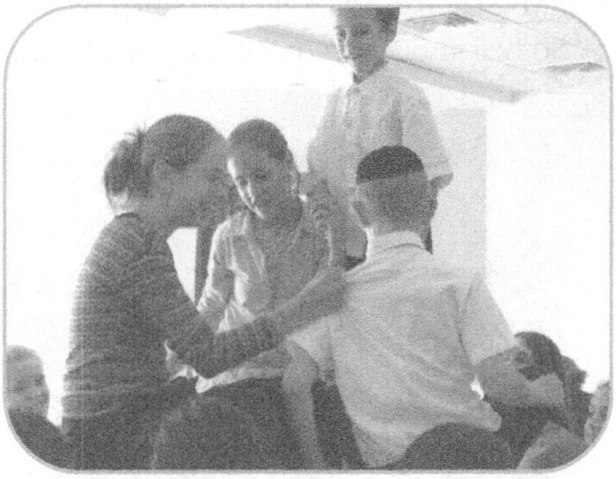

Lexi's bat mitzvah party in Israel

The year and a half passed much faster than we could have ever imagined. There were times that I was so impressed with ourselves and other times when I wondered what in the world we were doing and why. We made much effort in researching job opportunities (of which none were found), 220-volt appliance stores, shipping companies and possible communities to live in. As for communities, we waded through all sorts of information about the diverse cultural, religious and political atmospheres that were to be our reality in our new life, before deciding on Neve Daniel in the Gush Etzion region just south of Jerusalem. It didn't matter much; I wouldn't begin to really understand it all until I arrived.

Incredibly, Nefesh B'Nefesh received hundreds of applications in its inaugural year. Centered out of Boca Raton, there was much media attention to the history-making flight that was soon to be. In fact, months before the flight we began receiving calls from newspaper reporters requesting interviews. After one disappointing report Lawrence refused them all. He even had me cancel a TV interview for NBC!

One newspaper in particular just didn't give up. Finally we granted one last interview just to "get rid of them." A reporter and photojournalist came to our house. We thought they would do their interview, take some pictures, and that would be it. Boy, were we ever wrong! They didn't take any pictures that day. I don't even think it was the real interview. They came to plan a long-term arrangement where they would follow us and write a continuous report from that point until six months after our Aliyah date!

Somewhat surprised and more than a little concerned at how the articles would be slanted, I came up with an idea. We would agree to this as long as the two of them would promise to go, upon their arrival in Israel, to the Audio/Visual show on the history of Gush Etzion. What was most important to me was that they would appreciate what Gush Etzion is all about. I believe that anyone who actually understands Gush Etzion could only write positive material. Without any hesitation they both agreed.

So began our very public Aliyah adventure.

New homes in Neve Daniel

An Aliyah Journal

Moving Up

עליה

a·li·yah

(ä′lē-ä′), n.

1. rise, ascent, going up.
2. Immigration to Israel.

1

Moving...

Journal Entry #1: Thursday, June 27

Storming The House

We are down to the last final bits of our preparation.

Yesterday the moving people came for day one out of two of our "lift" (how they refer to moving the contents of your home overseas). Four moving men came into our house and started packing up everything in sight.

And I mean everything!

We had to carefully watch to make sure things that weren't supposed to be sent on the lift didn't get packed. Like our passports, for example. Problem was, there were four of them and only two of us! And to make it more interesting, my cleaning lady and her son were here asking for instructions, a charity organization showed up for a donation pick-up, the Fed-Ex guy came, the lawn guy was mowing outside, and a reporter and photographer from our local paper, the Sun-Sentinel, were over. And this was all in the first half-hour or so!

I gave up on watching the packers and ran to Starbucks for a badly needed coffee.

Anyway, the day went well. By the end, they had packed up most of our house, except the master bedroom. I took the kids out for a little picture-taking mission so that they could photograph places of importance to them, to make a memory book. It went very well, and it was a good escape for us from the insanity in our house.

Today, they will finish packing up our house then I will leave with the kids and a lot of suitcases for NY. My husband, Lawrence, will join me next week, when we will be having a party to say goodbye to our family and friends.

Our flight to Israel is scheduled for July 8th.

Counting down...

Journal Entry #2: Friday, June 28

The First Departure

Just to wrap up the saga with the lift. Yesterday the moving crew was storming my house yet again. This time to finalize the packing and to load up the truck. Not your typical moving truck either. No cute catch phrases on the outside – just an ugly container on an 18 wheeler flatbed, I guess. Ugly! It sat in front of my house all day. They fit the stuff in like a can of sardines. Of course they couldn't fit the few pieces of plywood that Lawrence ran for at the last minute to Home Depot. (Anyone need a few pieces of plywood?)

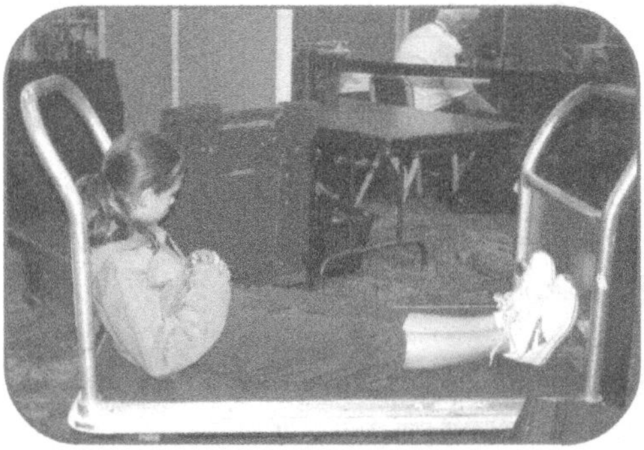

Lexi watching the luggage

Anyway, by around 2 p.m. I couldn't think of anything else to do. The rest of the family was out, and I was walking around in circles in my emptying house. It was a strange feeling. Of course I could have been following the movers around, then maybe Lawrence wouldn't have had to go running out to buy a shaver, having had his shaver packed by them!

Lucky for me, my kids and I left before the whole lift thing was done. Lawrence couldn't take me to the airport since he had to stay with the movers, so my sister-in-law and the Sun-Sentinel photographer took us to the airport. (Is this a story or what?) We packed pretty lightly with only eight over-stuffed pieces of luggage, each of which we could barely lift. We flew stand-by (never fly stand-by with eight pieces of overstuffed luggage and four kids) and here we are in NY.

Journal Entry #3: Sunday, June 30

Getting It All In

Wow... I am actually relaxed! If any of you ever plan to make Aliyah, I highly recommend making a pit-stop someplace in between the lift and the flight. I do feel a little bit guilty since Lawrence is still busy, busy, busy in Florida and I'm hanging out writing e-mails and playing with the color options.

Today we're doing some good, old-fashioned, American stuff. We had a big bar-b-que, and tonight we're going to watch the 4th of July fireworks. (I know it's only June 30th, but I guess the people here don't.)

I can almost forget that I am in the middle of a humongous move except that whenever I see people, they ask me about it.

Tomorrow I will drive up to Vermont to take the kids to say goodbye to my aunt and grandmother. That will certainly remind me of what it is that I am doing. Then we'll do some more, good, old-fashioned American stuff: a Yankee game! I guess we're just trying to get in as much as we can before we go and change our whole life.

Journal Entry #4: Monday, July 1

This Is For Real

I wasn't quite sure when it became official, but I suppose today pretty much sealed it: we closed on our house, and the contents of our home set sail for Israel. Though I'm about as detached from it as the rest of you since I am hanging out in my aunt's home in Vermont, relaxing and eating Ring Dings. On the way to my aunt's, we stopped at the Vermont nursing home where my grandmother is and had an emotional visit with her not knowing when the next time we would ever see her again. Tomorrow we're shooting to go to a Yankee game, but we have a 4 1/2 hour drive between us in Vermont and that Yankee game in the Bronx. Let's see our motivation!

Saying good-bye is not easy

Journal Entry #5: Friday, July 5

Final Events

I can't believe how fast this week is going! Yesterday was the goodbye party that my family made for us. It was great being able to see so many people, many of whom drove a great distance to be here. I thought my friends who drove from Lakewood, New Jersey came a long way, but then my cousins drove here all the way from Detroit, Michigan!

We're getting down to the wire. We've been running around shopping for stupid things whose sole purpose will be to make it completely impossible to close our luggage.

By the way, we did get to our baseball game. I made an interesting discovery about Yankee Stadium: There is no air-conditioning anywhere! (Even in the interior halls. What can I say? I've lived in Florida for nine years!) It was positively beastly there. Around 90 degrees at NIGHT. And so humid you could see the humidity! Of course we got there so late that we got nosebleeds on the way to our seats. Oh, and another thing about Yankee stadium: there is only one big screen to get info from and it was perfectly located in a spot that we couldn't see. But I DID go to the game, and they DID win.

Well, I've got to go do some more shopping now because I think I see an air pocket in one of my suitcases that I need to fill.

Journal Entry #6: Monday, July 8, 2:00 a.m.

Almost...

I can't believe it's July 8th! Our bags are basically packed (all 12 of them) and our carry-ons are like little suitcases. We somehow managed to take care of most of the things on our extremely long list.

I asked my boys what they were most excited about moving to Israel. Eight-year-old Eitan answered: "So I can go to the Western Wall again."

We really are leaving

Five-year-old Ezra answered: "To get a puppy and 'cause we're moving to the greatest house in the whole wide world." Not very spiritual, but at least he's excited.

We will be traveling to the airport in three cars. Two cars would be enough for our family and luggage. But not enough for all the people coming to send us off! We need to delay our "goodbyes" for as long as

My mom being interviewed at the airport

Emotional farewell

We're getting close, our plane is in sight

possible. None of us particularly like to say goodbye.

We are so excited to be on the first Nefesh B'Nefesh flight ever! It will be so amazing to be on an entire plane filled with people doing exactly what we are doing, and making history as we do it! I can't even imagine. But I don't need to because in a few short hours I will be part of it! I suppose I should try to get a good night's sleep. We will have our laptop computer with us so perhaps I can report to you from right in the thick of it all.

Anyway, thank you to everyone for all your good wishes, blessings and support (not to mention the warnings, pleas, threats and whoops! wasn't supposed to mention that!) Seriously, though, we could not have done this huge move without many of you (you know who you are) and we want you all to know that we appreciate everything.

Journal Entry #7: Tuesday, July 9

Wow!!!! What a flight! What a day!! What an experience!!!!!!!!!! As exhausted as I am, I feel that I just have to put down all of my thoughts because the longer I wait, the more diluted they become.

The Airport

I arrived with my family in 3 large vehicles with our 12 huge suitcases, and 6+ large carry-ons. As we pulled over to the curb, there were numerous other people with bazillions of suitcases as well. Our journey had begun. We arrived inside the El Al terminal to an incredible sight: There were blue and white balloons everywhere, press and media were out in full force. There were tons of people milling about. Right away one could sense the enormity of this event. After we checked our bags, the media people seemed to come out of the woodwork. My family interviewed with CNN, Associated Press, Gabe Pressman (NBC), and several others that either took photos or whatever. Not to mention our buddies from the Sun Sentinel. There was a big press conference that we stood right next to and watched, then, after cake and cookies (can you imagine? In JFK airport?) we proceeded to the security checkpoint. After lots of hugging, crying and stalling, we finally said goodbye to my family.

The Flight

First of all, I have never been on such a "short" flight to Israel. There was always something going on; everyone was so excited. We did some of our aliyah paperwork right on the plane. Wait a minute; I forgot to mention the seats: They had us in the first row of coach! The three seats you are

Filling out our Ministry of Interior paperwork on the plane

looking at the moment you step in the plane. Besides that it's a bulkhead seat with more legroom than business class, it's also an emergency exit row. Most flights would not place a couple with 4 young kids in an emergency row. But this was no ordinary flight. Needless to say, we did not get much sleep on this plane. There were also lots of media people on the flight who

Finally seeing Israel... The emotions were high!

could at any moment be taking pictures or filming you. Anyway, the flight was truly great. Everyone was very friendly, helped each other out, and really got along great.

Binyamin Netanyahu greeting me on arrival

The Arrival

After we'd landed and taxied toward our stopping point, we started to clearly see the crowds that would be greeting us shortly. CROWDS! It seemed that a huge number of them were from the press and the media. They pulled our plane up to the two staircases that let you off, and had our family exit from the front with the 1st class/VIP group. The difference with the two is that our staircase was overflowing with the media, and had waiting for us at the bottom, none other than Binyamin Netanyahu. What a thrill! He personally greeted me and my entire family, shook our hands, and the whole experience made us feel like a million bucks. Then, as we continued on our way through the crowds, cameras and microphones were pushed into our faces from every direction. "Why did you move?" and "Are you afraid of the situation?" and "Where are you from?" were asked by dozens(?) of reporters. Did you ever see clips of the Beatles arriving in the States for the first time? Well that's what it reminded me of. Anyway, then there was the special welcome ceremony. It was truly beautiful and moving. And again, cameras and reporters approaching like mad. I only hope that whatever I did say to any of those reporters came out right and was reported well. A sample of those who interviewed us is ABC, London Times, Newsweek and People Magazine (or maybe those two were the same person?) There was also an in-Hebrew interview that I did miserably at, but at least I tried!!!

2

Arriving...

Journal Entry #8: Wednesday, July 10

I am still without an internet connection. What a primitive life I am living right now!! Actually, it is quite amazing how the children find all new ways to entertain themselves when they are deprived of TV, VCR, computer, internet, radio, etc. It's a little like camping. In fact, we don't even have a microwave! But don't start feeling bad for us just yet: we're doing great. Let's see, where did I leave off? Oh yes, so we arrived.

As new *olim* (immigrants) we are provided with a free ride to our first destination. Unfortunately, they didn't have their act together on coordinating the rides to Gush Etzion. To make a long story short, we ended up stuffing all of our things into and onto a cab, rode it to Jerusalem, then sat and waited in intense heat for half an hour waiting for a bus to come and take us to Gush Etzion –at which time we had to unstuff the cab and load up the bus. We did have two very kind helpers – the Sun-Sentinel reporters!

Arrival At Neve Daniel

About the best part of that whole episode was sitting next to my 11-year-old daughter, Lexi, as we were nearing the Gush, and she, my most reluctant oleh, couldn't wait to see Neve Daniel! She was bursting with excitement!! Thank G-d that excitement has only grown. In fact, my children have spent more hours in the past two days playing with other children than normally occurred in a week. But more on that later.

Anyway, so we arrived at the house – here's the scenario. We are all totally exhausted, yet exhilarated, by the events of the preceding 24 hours. There are several adults and children waiting to greet us at the house, the reporter and photographer from the Sun Sentinel are accompanying us, and we arrive at the house for the first time. I have to say that it was a bit shocking for both Lawrence and me. We felt obligated to keep up a good

Lawrence putting up the screens

face especially since our reaction would be reported. But the reality is that we were stunned. First of all, cosmetically the house looked nothing like when I had selected it in May. We expected this, since it was beautifully furnished then, and had a lovely garden with many potted plants, all of which we knew in advance they would be taking. What we had not realized was there were no screens in the house, (and no air conditioning which wouldn't be a problem if there were screens!) Unfortunately we arrived during a heat wave. The choices became: Windows closed, less bugs and a stiflingly hot house; or windows open, more bugs and a slightly less stiflingly hot house. It did not make us happy. After a very sleepless night we awoke in our hot, buggy house with some mosquito bites as souvenirs. My friend (we make friends fast here) Ariela was going to Jerusalem for errands. I joined her and was thrilled to discover her errand was to the Home Center (like Home Depot). I bought ten meters of screening material, a hot glue gun, a bug zapper and some fans. The only problem was that our errands went overtime and I found myself running late for an appointment with – Bob Jamieson (or it might be Bill – I keep forgetting), a foreign news correspondent for Peter Jennings on ABC.

Network News

The problem was that I arrived laden with my heavy bags, very much not camera-ready (read: I looked horrible). I walked in to find the camera crew all set up and filming my sweaty arrival. So I took off and fixed up a bit. We then spent the next two+ hours with the ABC crew. The thing was that we expected it to take only an hour; because immediately after we had scheduled with Gabe Pressman and NBC! So we had a whole NBC crew waiting for over an hour to do their interview!!! One of the reasons it took so long is that the ABC people thought that filming us hot-gluing a screen to our window would make for very profitable news.

So then the next interview started. I have to say, these interviews got way too political for us. We were extremely uncomfortable and I know that I said things that will not go over well with the general TV audiences. Also, we were not aware of the whole "sound bite" concept with news broadcasts where individual thoughts and phrases are left intact so that each phrase/ sentence you say should be a complete "sound bite" so that if the phrase before or after is deleted, your idea will not be distorted too badly. I apologize in advance for anything that doesn't come out right on the news.

Our Hike

Hiking up to the makolet

After all of the TV crews left, it was time to take the boys on the hike we had promised them. The girls were long gone with friends, so we went with the boys, oh, and our Sun Sentinel buddies, and started to "hike" to the *makolet* (local market: the only store in town). I call it a hike because it is up such a steep incline, that you can't just say walking "up the block". It's a microscopic place that you would certainly miss if you didn't know what to look for, but it has what we need and the owner is nice. We bought some very exciting things like water and tehina. We checked out the park nearby, and then we went home.

Journal Entry #9: Thursday, July 11

A Normal Day?

A relatively normal day – at least more normal than the last two. I was up at 5 a.m. – in time to see the swirling fog that seems to be a standard event in Neve Daniel. It was like G-d had placed a heavy veil on my view, a veil that was blowing in the wind to allow teasing glimpses here and there. Not to worry – my beautiful view was back in time for my 7 a.m. walk to the makolet with Ezra. You want to hear small-town? At the makolet the proprietor offered for me to open an account that could be paid once a month. I gladly opened it and he gave me the number to my account. Are you ready? My number is 5. I better write that down in case I forget.

Sound and Light Show

Neither of my girls was home since they had slept over at friends' houses (on only the second night!). Now that we'd become somewhat settled (superficially at least) we wanted to take the time to go to the Gush Etzion Sound and Light Show. It's somewhat of a misnomer, as it is more of a multimedia film experience. It is a very important piece that illustrates the history of Gush Etzion and highlights its importance to Israel and to her people. We wanted to bring all of the children, but the girls were not home. We decided to go anyway, because we were going with Tim and Mike, the journalists who are doing the series on our aliyah. We did not think it was fair to expect them to accurately report without access to all of the information. So we took them (they took us?) to the show. It was very moving for us, and I think for them too. I'm very glad we went with them.

Busy, Busy, Busy

What else happened today? We registered three of the kids for school, we rented a car (yes!), Lexi started a mosaics activity with other kids, 12-year-old Shira went on another sleepover – with Hebrew-speaking Israelis(!), Eitan went to a late-night campfire event, with roasted marshmallows and the works, and Ezra just stayed home and played with his favorite friend so far: Mike, the Sun-Sentinel photographer.

Journal Entry #10: Sunday, July 14

I cannot believe it is Sunday already!! Well, we finally got an internet connection for a brief time – too brief to send anything but enough to at least view and listen to some of the press coverage of the unbelievable event that we were blessed to be a part of.

I have to say that I am incredibly happy. Our first *Shabbos* (Sabbath, also Shabbat) here was wonderful. The people here were so friendly to us; they brought us cake, they introduced themselves, and children came over to play with our kids. It was wonderful.

Anyway, today we started the process of joining mainstream life in Israel. We opened a bank account, and applied for medical insurance.

In the afternoon we did the most important thing. We took the children to the Kotel (Western Wall). I must say that the experience today was different than any other time I'd been there. Of course the Kotel is ours, and special, and has meaning to any Jew who comes. However, when we came today it was not as tourists as it had been in the past. All of a sudden we were there as Israelis – we live here. There was no longer any element of being a

A celebration at the Kotel

tourist, just purely the element of ownership. Being at the most holy place to us in the world, and WE LIVE HERE! We can go there whenever we want to! That is so incredible!!!! The children all had an opportunity to learn the significance of the Wall and what it represents to us. We had them each put on a shirt of their own and tear it (*keriah*) as soon as they saw the wall as a reminder of what once was (the Beit Hamikdash or Temple) and that we are awaiting the rebuilding of it. Each child tore his/her shirt with no complaints.

Journal Entry #11: Tuesday, July 16

The Aliyah Trend

I was just talking to my sister about the small effects that the Nefesh B'Nefesh aliyah is having on future aliyah and she said "Not small effects, big effects." What an incredible thing we have been a part of. I want to recall for you a conversation I had with a friend one year ago. A day or so before leaving for Israel last summer, I was with the kids in a pizza place in Florida. I ran into someone I hadn't seen in a very long time and we were catching each other up on our lives. I told her we were planning on making Aliyah. Do you know how she answered? She said, "Oh, people still do that?" Can you imagine? Like it was some kooky trend in the seventies that went out with lava lamps and bell bottoms.

Now fast forward one whole year. Four hundred people just made aliyah with an organization that didn't exist one year ago. People who never would have thought of making aliyah are all of a sudden thinking about it. And many people are really doing it. When I've told people recently that I was making aliyah, the responses have been more along the lines of "Oh, my friends are going too," or "You are living my dream, I want to go."

Teudat Zehut

Guess what we got yesterday?? Our teudot zehut! (Identity cards). For those of you who don't know, receiving an Israeli identity card is one of those things that is preceded by several waits in long lines. By going on the Nefesh B'Nefesh flight, the first long line came to us; we had three people from the Interior Ministry who were actually on our plane processing the forms. The next line came to us as well – though we're not sure as to exactly how!! Yesterday morning there was a knock at our door; one of the kids answered it, and then came to me holding our identity cards. Can you imagine? Hand delivered to my door! By whom, I have no idea.

Hitchhikers

One of the unique things about living in a small, closed community in Israel is that hitchhiking is normal. Basically, one will go to the bus stop and wait for whichever comes first: a bus, or a car going in the same direction.

This is done by young and old alike, kind of like very informal carpool. The other day I was traveling to Jerusalem with a friend and she picked up a family of five "tremping" (hitchhiking) at the bus stop. And this is normal!

Our Oven

Actually, that title is a misnomer since we don't actually have an oven. In Israel, when you move you take your appliances as well. However the family we're renting from was going to leave the oven and stove for us for whatever reason. To make a long story short, we didn't buy one, and they didn't leave one! So now we are looking for an oven, and ovens are popping out of the woodwork. Our neighbor shlepped over an oven (these are built-ins by the way, with separate stove tops) and we tried to squash the stove top into the space but it didn't fit. Someone else in the neighborhood happens to have an extra oven that she won, but it does not include a stovetop. Shopping for food is very interesting since I must buy foods to prepare without the use of an oven or a stove. But do not fret since for those of you who know me well, I always find what to eat!

This Paragraph Is For The Dogs

As we've been gearing up for our big move, each family member has been excited about one thing or another. (The Western Wall, the schools, the view, etc.) Ezra, however, has been excited for one thing: getting a puppy. Problem was, we weren't getting a puppy. Not as far as his Dad was concerned. Yet an interesting phenomenon has been taking place. Everyone we talk to recommends getting a dog! Even the guy in charge of security on

The Samoyed

the yishuv told us to get a dog. So you know what? I think we're getting a dog. Our only problem is we're all thinking about a smallish-medium sized dog, and Lawrence is more in favor of a horse-sized dog. (By the way, any good suggestions for a family dog that will do double-duty as a watch dog?)

Another thing about dogs: Lexi. My Lexi has wanted a dog as well. Problem is she wouldn't even go into someone's house if they had a dog. Well, everyone, the impossible has taken place: her new best friend has a Samoyed (BIG dog). Thanks to a little breaking-in at my Aunt's house in Vermont (with her little cock-a-poos), she was less fearful than she would have been in the past. She now pets and walks this huge dog! (Aunt Wittie, are you so proud of her?)

By the way, anyone ever hear of a Great Pyrenees? That's the dog Lawrence wants.

Journal Entry #12: Wednesday, July 17

Tisha B'Av Night At The Herodian

Doesn't that sound like a great thing to do on Tisha B'Av (the saddest day of the year mourning the loss of the Temple among other major things)? The significance of the Herodian for those of you who don't know (and I'd have included myself up to a few hours ago) is it was the summer get-away palace for King Herod. King Herod also contributed to the final construction of the second Temple, so the Herodian was a contemporary structure to the Temple. We're talking 2,000 years ago, by the way. Anyway, Herodian is fairly close to Jerusalem, and is at a high altitude so that you can technically see the Temple Mount

The Herodian

from Herodian. Since Herodian is in Gush Etzion, it is the traditional place for residents to go on Tisha B'Av. Sounds great? It wasn't great. Perhaps I should have realized it was a bad idea when they told me the time of departure was 7:35 p.m. and I most likely wouldn't get my boys to bed by their 8 p.m. bedtime. I guess I'm not that smart. I got very caught up in doing every single thing that came up, and this sounded so cool! It was very cool – for the other people. It really wasn't that bad. Some exciting things were the really cool night-vision scopes that the army guys were using, and while everyone else was listening to *Eicha*, I was entertaining the boys by having them search by flashlight for some archaeologically significant things. The significant things we found were a button (likely lost that very evening) and a real bone. Anyway, that was Tisha B'Av night at the Herodian.

Ezra WILL Go To School

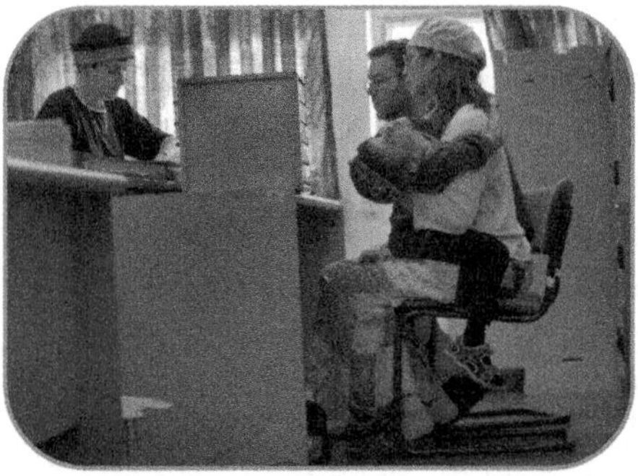

Signing up Ezra for school

After several unsuccessful attempts, Ezra is officially registered at school! We had been going to Efrat daily to sign him up and at first we were sent from one location to another. We finally found the right location yesterday, but the woman was out for the day! Anyhow, today she was there, and the sign up is complete.

Camp Counselor For An Hour

The woman who was leading Eitan's round-robin camp today had to be out for about an hour and asked me to cover for her. Yikes!! Fifteen wild third graders who don't speak English! I tried reading them a story. Those of you who know me well know that that is something I enjoy and can keep kids attention with. Not in Hebrew! I finally took them outside for some good, old-fashioned basketball which kept them very happy.

Journal Entry #13: Friday, July 19

Our Shabbos Meal

It is Erev Shabbos, about 1 hour before the start of Shabbos. As you know, this community is quite hospitable and people have been having us over for nearly every meal, particularly the Shabbos meals. A very nice family was appointed to be our "adoptive" family, to help us with many things, one of which is coordinating our meals. Everything was going just fine until today. You see, the family that we were expecting to eat at tonight never said anything to us. As the week went by we started to wonder if we were expected there after all. Guess what – we were not expected there! Luckily, I called my adoptive family and she made the uncomfortable call to discover that they were not planning on having us tonight. Back to this being a very hospitable neighborhood: the few people involved with figuring out the situation all offered to have us over tonight, so we are quite set. By the way, it's not like I would have minded just eating home tonight, except that we STILL don't have an oven or stove!

Kids' Activities

It seems that there is no shortage of things for kids to do in this area. On Wednesday the girls went horseback riding on a nearby moshav, Rosh Tzurim. The view from there was so unbelievable! They had a wonderful time. Eitan finished the round-robin camp he was going to.

On Sunday Eitan will be going to a camp in Gush Etzion that is supposed to be fantastic. Ezra will start at a nearby camp run by neighborhood girls. And on Monday Shira and Lexi are going to sleep-away camp! Problem is we decided and registered TODAY. So we have Sunday to shop, prepare, and pack for both girls. Luckily, it's only one week, but it's still sleep-away.

Rental Cars And Borrowed Cars

Last Thursday we rented a car for a week. While we were no closer to buying a car today than last week, it was quite an expense and we wanted to return the car. Know what happened? Our neighbor just happened to hear that we need a car, and they just happen to be going away for a week, so they brought their car over, gave us the keys, and now we have a car for another week!

Crew Has Been Cut

One of the things we needed to do before our big move was give the three boys badly needed haircuts. We figured that on the priority list that wasn't very high. So we decided this was something we could do in Monsey. Except that we were leaving on the first day of the three week period that we CAN'T GET HAIRCUTS! Oh well, too bad for us. By this morning Lawrence and the boys looked like grizzly bears. I cut their hair right outside our house without a comb (our combs are on the lift). They all look good despite the lack of a comb.

Journal Entry #14: Monday, July 22 or "Line by Line"

What A Feeling!

We went to Yerushalayim again today, this time to get through some of the bureaucratic stuff. Besides for all the departments we went to, (more about that later) Lawrence and I trekked all over the center of Jerusalem. At one point I stopped walking and pointed out everything to Lawrence and said "You see all this? We live here!" It is such an incredible feeling!

Bureaucracy

First on our agenda today was our driver's license. When you make Aliyah, you have three months to get your driver's license the less difficult way. After three months it becomes the more difficult way. We decided to make it a priority. We first went to Israel's version of the AAA (called MEMSI) for our picture to be taken. The photos were being taken in a little basement room. We arrived there and found about ten people sitting in chairs, and maybe 3 or 4 on line. So we lined up behind them. When the last person before us had just gone, someone else got up right in front of us. "The nerve!" I thought and was about to assert myself when someone pointed out that she was before me and that when you arrive you have to ask "Who is last" and then pay attention and go after that person. "Aha, so that's how it is here," I said to myself.

That's NOT How It Is Here

Next we went across the street for our eye tests and physical exams. There we followed the line pretty well. I couldn't figure out the eye test machine so, believe it or not, I cheated on that test. (Afterwards Lawrence told me that he had her ADJUST the machine and that's probably all I needed, too). Thank G-d, I got a clean bill of health at my physical exam. I told the doctor that I didn't understand the questionnaire but that I didn't have any health problems. He marked "No" at every question, and signed it, just like that. He didn't even have to touch me! If you want to be cured of any ailment, just go to a Driver's License Bureau doctor in Israel.

Then we walked across town to the next stop. We arrived and found a large number of people there before us. Luckily, this place had a "Take-a-number" system. A large sign directed us to take a number –"43" we read. We saw that they were up to "31". At this point we were quite hungry so Lawrence sat and waited and I searched for food. I came back (empty-handed) and we went in to check what number they were up to. Then we realized that there was another digit in the system – they were at 331. And we had 443! We quickly realized that there was neither a number system, nor even a line. We presented ourselves at the counter and were helped immediately. Things seemed to be going well until she handed us our papers and told us to go somewhere to make photocopies of our US licenses and the papers and then to return the next day. I quickly mentioned that we had copies of our licenses, would that help? It did! Their copy machine was broken, but with our copied license, the rest she could copy by fax. Now all we have left to do is take two driving lessons and our driving tests. (I'm not joking, we really have to do that!)

The Last Line Of The Day

We hiked some more over to Jerusalem Bank to register for the rental subsidy we are entitled to. This was a really strange experience. This line actually was a "take-a-number" line. (We got 100, they were on 84). The department we went to is the same department that deals with home mortgages. The majority of the people in the room with us were Arabs. Here we were in the Bank of Jerusalem, getting our special Aliyah benefits, and we were waiting in a room full of Arabs. Not the guys with masks shooting Uzis in the air; there were young couples with small children, older women perhaps with their grown children, lots of babies and little kids. We had quite a wait so I had lots of time to contemplate the whole thing. First of all, we are more or less at war. Yet here were those very people we are at war with getting mortgages in our banks. I looked around at the faces. Could I personally be responsible for any harm to come to them had I the chance? Absolutely not. But how would they respond given the reverse opportunity? Good question that I wouldn't want to ask. I looked at a little baby girl, maybe 16 months, sitting with her mom right in front of me. I caught her eye and I smiled at her. Would she smile back? I thought of her innocence and wondered what the future would bring her. Would she learn to hate me? Or not? I tried not to imagine that some of the suicide bombers were once cute little Arab girls like her. Maybe she read my mind because instead of a smile her face started to quake in that I'm-about-to-cry-really-loud face. She didn't just cry; She looked at me, wailed and looked back at her mom. Over and over! Like she was trying to tell her mother that it's my fault! Luckily a manager happened to come and pulled us out of the line before our turn.

The moral to all of this? Never judge a line by its number.

Journal Entry #15: Tuesday, July 23

Crash Test Dummies

Well, another fun-filled, adventure-packed day. We spent the morning in Talpiot, furniture shopping. We had some spare time, and decided to check out some car dealerships. The first one we saw was a Volkswagen dealer. Lawrence was reluctant since it is a German car dealer. I told him that we are living in a country that hires the very people we are at war against since the labor is cheaper, and we're worrying about buying German? Anyway, we saw the Volkswagen Caravelle. It's very nice, seats 9 people, and costs a lot of money. In fact it seats so many that we were told we would get a tax break since it is considered a "private bus."

Eitan and Ezra at entrance to Kef-Tzuba

Next we went to Citroen to see the Jumpy. This one is considered the best deal on a similar-sized vehicle. It's also ugly, sparsely fitted, and has a commercial feel to it. Anyway, we asked the dealer about its safety record. He said that no one has done crash tests on the Jumpy. I then asked how it has fared in actual crashes since the Jumpy is apparently a popular car, and crashes seem to be pretty popular here too. Sorry, he told us, but he doesn't know of anyone who crashed a Jumpy.

Wax Skating

This afternoon our friends were going to a place called "Kef-Tzoba", an outdoor amusement place for kids. We decided to follow them there. We took one of their cell phones, the kind you can use as a walkie-talkie. Then they led us through a very scenic back road and gave us a guided tour with the walkie-talkie. Great route! We saw parts of Jerusalem that we'd never seen, or simply never seen in that way, such as Haddasah-Ein Kerem Hospital from the valley below.

Anyway we got to this place and the kids had a blast. It had all the inflatable stuff that you jump in and on. Miss Energy that I am, I had to do this stuff too. I scrambled to the top of this slide thing with my sons, then tried to hold my skirt modestly as I tumbled down to the bottom. No one told me you have to wear socks – I actually got a small second-degree burn from the friction. Can you imagine? Well, that was it for me. Until I realized there was skating inside. A quite bizarre form of skating if you ask me, with regular ice skates and a sort of wax coated floor instead of ice. Two obstacles though: I had no socks and I had this stupid burn on my foot. Easy enough. I borrowed Lawrence's (sweaty – Ugh!) socks and determined that there would be less friction on my foot while it was protected by the sock and skate, than not. It was actually kind of fun, though I think my left skate blade needed an alignment.

Now I'm Really Cooking

No, I don't have an oven yet but I do have this little thing, about the size of a small microwave that cooks. I decided it's time to start cooking. I bought the ingredients for a squash kugel, and began to make it tonight. It was going great until I started to pour the flour. In Israel people sift their flour in case there is a tiny bug. My sifter is on a boat crossing some exotic body of water right now, so I figured I would just pour the flour slowly into a bowl and check it that way. Well, I'll skip the middle of the story – and go straight to the end. (You don't want to know the middle!) I threw out the flour, and borrowed more from a neighbor – and a sifter!!

Journal Entry #16: Wednesday, July 24

Kosher Food – Israeli Style

My kids wanted to use our landlord's microwave. (We are only occupying the upstairs part of the house until August 6th, and she has lots of stuff downstairs). We told them we can't since we don't know if it's kosher. Eitan said, "It is kosher. She made us popcorn in it and she saw we were wearing kippas"

Scary Part Of Living Here

Aha! Your eyes perked up? Waiting to hear the real scoop? Well the real scoop is not what you think. Some animal nearby howls at the moon. You know – that werewolf noise. Come on, wouldn't that scare you too? I'm not going out at night! I think it's time to get that dog...

It's Curtains For Us

Since we got here our lives have been open to the world via the media, and to Neve Daniel via our windows! We decided it's time to put something on our windows besides just screens. Before we moved in, the landlord had these cool, Persian things hanging that we liked very much. A few days after we got here, we were in the Old City and we found a store that sold them. We went back there today and negotiated poorly and bought a bunch of them. One day you'll all get to see our poor negotiation skills since the whole transaction was filmed by the guys doing the documentary on Nefesh B'Nefesh.

What's In A Name?

For any of you who don't watch the news, we are using our "alias" here in Israel. Actually, our name "Welch" has to be so distorted when written in Hebrew that it would never be spelled or pronounced correctly. Since our last name comes from Lawrence's father, we decided to use his first name instead: "Ben-David" (literally, "the son of David"). We are also using our Hebrew names on all legal documents in Israel. So officially here we are Ariella and Chaim Ben-David. We are still introducing ourselves as Laura and Lawrence and will continue to do so. We are keeping "Welch" on all American documents, except for what may come in the mail. Our mail lady is confused enough since there are no street names or numbers.

Journal Entry #17: Friday, July 26

The Lift Has Landed

Yesterday was the big day we had been planning for days. We would pick up the boys early from camp and set out for Netanya to go to the big Ikea store and shop for furniture. We planned and coordinated, as we had a limited time since Visiting Day for the girls in Kfar Saba was at 5:30 p.m. that same day. As we were getting ready to leave, we received a phone call from Gamma Shipping (the Israeli end of Omega Shipping that shipped our stuff).

"Your lift is here," the guy, whose name was Guy incidentally, announced. "You need to come to Ashdod to sign the documents."

"Great," my husband answered. "Can we come on Sunday?"

"No, you need to come today. After the weekend we start charging you a storage fee."

Well, that was the end of Ikea. We quickly regrouped, grabbed every one of the not-very-good maps we own, and headed to Ashdod. Actually, we went to Yavneh which is near Ashdod. Success! We went via a scenic route through Gefen and Tirosh (wine country) and got to our destination, papers signed and all. In fact we even had time to go to Hertzliyah beach before visiting the girls at their camp. We didn't buy furniture, but we had an awesome day.

Manual Cars, Shots, And Other Awful Stuff

Today we had an appointment for Driving Lesson #1 (out of 2). My husband found out that if we don't take the lessons/test with a manual shift car, then our license will exclude manual cars. Knowing he was right I consented though I was not happy about it. (It's been years since I regularly drove a stick-shift car, and even then I was never that good at it.) Anyway, we meet the guy (his name was NOT Guy) in Jerusalem and it was time to begin. Without a doubt Lawrence had to go first. At least I could see what was coming. Well, let me tell you, this torture lasted FORTY MINUTES. Each!! (I think mine was longer!) While Lawrence had his turn through narrow one-way streets with heavy traffic, ridiculously sharp turns, and HILLS (stick shift!) I sat back, watched the scenery go by, and PANICKED! I actually entertained the thought that I would rather get a shot in the rear then do the stupid driving lesson with this guy. (You need to realize that although this was not the test, the teacher is the one to decide if you qualify to take it. We know of people with limo licenses who were not recommended for the test!) I started noticing all sorts of ailments that perhaps I should use as an excuse to get out of this lesson.

Finally, the time came for my turn. I slowly organized all of my mirrors, and tested out the gears. Oops! I elbowed the instructor right in the gut when I tested reverse. And why, exactly, was I putting the car in reverse if I needed to go forward, he wanted to know. Just testing the gears, I sheepishly replied. And then, I was off. You know, I put so much energy into concentrating on the instructions, shifting, clutching, breaking and trying not to do all at the same time, that my time actually felt like it went faster than Lawrence's did.

The best part of this whole story: the guy felt that our driving was so good that we could skip the second lesson if we wanted to. If we WANTED to? Is the Pope Catholic? We wanted to.

By The Way

I mentioned the other day that we went to the Old City to shop for curtains. I forgot to mention that shortly after we arrived I made another of my astonishing discoveries related to the fact that we are not tourists: I was in the old city and I was not holding a camera. The important thing to note here is that it was NOT a light and liberating feeling as one would expect. It was annoying and irritating as perfect shot after perfect shot passed before my eyes with no camera to capture it. It did one thing for us though. We have been holding off on a purchase of either a digital camera or digital video camera since we could not decide which to get. Now I know we need the digital camera. It will save us a lot of money on film and developing for all of the trillions of pictures that I take, most of which could then be deleted with the touch of a button!

Journal Entry #18: Sunday, July 28

The Not-So-Light Light Show

As basically an optimist, I've been telling you all sorts of great things about our move. This is not to say that it has not been great, because it has. However, different people view things differently and may paint a different picture of similar things. Not everything is great, though, and I would be dishonest if I only told you the good things.

On Friday night we were over at our neighbors for the Friday night meal. Before entering the house we saw what looked like an extremely bright star in the horizon. Our neighbor, Raffi, told us it was a "light bomb". This is something like military fireworks that gets shot up into the air, and stays lit for a while (seconds? minutes?) and is able to light a huge area, usually for some type of search. Anyway, we were all fascinated and stayed outside watching as several of these things went up one after the other then slowly fizzled out and fell out of the sky. Unfortunately, the next morning we found out that the source of our "entertainment" was a massive search for the ones who murdered a husband and wife and one of their ten children on the road someplace near Hebron.

This is a short journal as I am feeling a bit under the weather right now. I've got a bad case of "New Environment Germs." It has been going through my household in various forms, but it feels like the flu to me. Lawrence went out on his first solo errand trip since we got here because I felt so lousy. (Actually all of our outings together have been great – this is almost like a second honeymoon!) Anyway, I'm going to go lie down and read Harry Potter in Hebrew.

Journal Entry #19: Monday, July 29

Fans And Curtains

Okay, everyone, the honeymoon is over. Lawrence has been working on getting fans and curtains up almost since we got here. He would go to Home Center daily because what he would get was just a little bit off. Today was the day that those fans and those stupid curtains were going up no matter what. Wrong! The curtains that we put so much time and effort in selecting (and bought too far away to return) were the wrong size. All of them. With so many windows in the house, how could we mess up on so many? The fans have been extremely challenging. Lawrence finally figured out how to get the special cement bolts?/screws? into the ceiling, when OOPS! Something happened that caused the darn things to get stuck halfway in, and they wouldn't budge. In the meantime we're having a heat wave and the house is broiling. Lawrence plopped down on the couch and said "I give up!" Of course I was no help since I was in bed all day – broiling as well. But you know what? For all that we're going through, at least we're going through it in ISRAEL.

KidSpeak

My daughter Lexi made a great comment today. She said, "I don't get why people say that they are so 'jealous' of us making Aliyah. If they feel that way, they should pack up and make Aliyah too!" Right on Lexi!

Perfectly Scheduled Week – Israeli-Style

What a full week we had planned! We expected calls on Sunday from our driving instructor, to confirm our driving tests on Monday, and from the shipping company to confirm our lift delivery on Wednesday. Then, of course, we had Tuesday to empty the house of the borrowed items to make room for our stuff. So, no one called on Sunday, and we couldn't get a hold of any of them. (Remember, here Sunday is a regular workday). Monday we spoke to Guy (Remember him? From the shipping company?) and he had no information. We spoke to the driving instructor and he scheduled our tests for Wednesday at 7:10 a.m. Right, I was as surprised as you are. It was a bad connection and I made him repeat it ten times, because surely I had misheard him. What kind of a crazy time is that to take a driving test?!?! Oh, and as far as emptying the house, the truck that is used by the community is unavailable until – THE MIDDLE OF NEXT WEEK! We were instructed to simply bring all of the furniture outside and leave it there until they get the truck. I guess we won't be having company any time soon.

The Girls Have Returned

After a week in sleep-away camp, Shira and Lexi are home. It was a mostly positive experience for them, and they met many people and did some really fun things. (Certainly more fun than going to Home Center!) Now they have returned to their horseback riding lessons.

Journal Entry #20: Tuesday, July 30

Tennis Anyone?

Lawrence has found a new contact sport that he enjoys, though I don't know how much exercise he gets from it. We got a really cool tennis racquet-looking thing from Aubergine, my aunt's store in Vermont, that actually has an electric charge. You chase around the bug, and when it lands on the racquet, ZAP!! Of course for me it is merely a spectator sport.

Eitan settles in with basketball

Unusual Day

As I was still feeling quite under the weather today, and we are experiencing a dreadful heat wave (Remember: no A/C!) Lawrence thought I would be better off at our friends house recuperating. Boy, was he right! They had all these unusual amenities like Air Conditioning, TV, VCR, not to mention Chicken Soup (which was probably the most important thing!) Seriously though, it's been only a few weeks and I forgot that I always had the above mentioned items. By the way, I found out what this virus that I've got is called: "Arafat's Revenge."

Big Day Is Coming

Tomorrow I had better be 100% better because I am going to be super busy! First we need to be in Jerusalem at 7:10 a.m. for the driving test. Then we need to prepare for the arrival of our lift (which we have done nothing to prepare for). It's not like we haven't done anything. Lawrence is still working on those darn fans. (I asked him if he will be naming them when he is through). OK, I guess I haven't really done anything (besides watch a great movie) but I had an excuse!

Next Chapter On Our Oven

The oven that's been sitting on our kitchen floor is now installed, cleaned and made kosher. Unfortunately we still don't have a price on it so we're not sure if we're keeping it! At least I can cook in the meantime.

Late Breaking News!

Lawrence has completely put together and installed exactly ONE fan. And . . . it works!! Great job, Lawrence!

Journal Entry #21: Wednesday, July 31

Can We Redo Wednesday On Thursday?

Oh man, this one is a doozy. Remember our jam-packed day scheduled for today? Driver's test at 7:10 a.m. and then the lift arriving? Well let's backtrack to the night before: I'm up most of the night with viral symptoms. I finally get to sleep around 5 a.m., only to be woken by the alarm at 5:30, for Lawrence to go to daven (pray) at the very early minyan (prayer service). Lawrence suggests that maybe I skip the test and do it a different day, but Oh, no. I'm going to do it when it's scheduled! So I drag myself out of bed and get ready to go.

We were leaving Neve Daniel when we passed people looking for a ride to Talpiot (S.E. Jerusalem) where we were going for the driver's tests anyway. Shortly after we had picked them up I went over the conversation I had with the driving instructor (who set the appointment for the exam) in my mind just one more time to make sure there could be no mistake about the 7:10 am test. I remembered distinctly he had said Wednesday, August 1st.

Whoops! It's July 31st. Did he mess up the date or did I? I thought harder and remembered he hadn't used the word Wednesday, he said *Yom Chamishi*, or the fifth day of the week. What an idiot I was! How come I could remember the conversation clear as day on the wrong day when we were rushing to a test that wasn't about to happen, but I could never process it properly any time before then? Maybe it's that darn virus? Well, here we were, riding along, with people in the car who were expecting a ride to Talpiot, and I had to 'fess up to Lawrence.

I broke it to him very gently. Maybe it was a good thing there were witnesses in the car? We delivered our passengers to their destination, and just to make sure the excursion was a total loss, we made two more pointless stops. One, to go to a hotel to pick up a package that wasn't there; and the other to go to the Unemployment Office in Jerusalem which was closed. But we always have to look at the bright side: #1, the people whose car we borrowed still haven't returned (we thought they were coming back on Sunday) and #2, the car has air conditioning!!! (It's a million degrees today). Oh, and by the way, the lift is not coming until tomorrow.

The Checks Were Not In The Mail...

...but they were at the bank!! Lawrence picked up our brand new Israeli checks today. We'd been waiting for over two weeks for them to arrive, when it occurred to us that that just may never happen. On his way out he remembered that we'd ordered MasterCards too. Yup, they were there! If you don't ask, you don't get. That seems to be a common motto here. Anyway, we were very excited to get the checks and the cards. Kind of a consolation prize for not getting our driver's licenses!

Progress In The House

The second fan is now fully installed and functional and the curtains on the big living-room windows are almost ready to be hung. We're getting there! (Just wait until the avalanche of stuff from a 40-ft container gets crammed into our little house. That's when we'll really get started!)

Journal Entry #22: Thursday, August 1

And Now For The Big Question: Did We Pass The Driver's Test???

That's a really good question, I'm so glad you asked. We don't know yet if Lawrence passed the test. But I definitely did not pass the test. That is because I did not take the test. After snoozing our alarm every five minutes from 5:30 a.m .to 6:35 a.m., finally we got up in a rush. We left at the very punctual time of 7:02 a.m. for a 7:10 a.m. test in Jerusalem. OK, nobody's perfect! We sped there and were about 7 minutes late. We called to let them know we were running late, we apologized profusely when we got there, but to no avail. We were naughty and the driver's test guy felt obligated to punish us. With thick accent: "Soh-ry! You late, only wan ahf you take test!" We couldn't believe it! Didn't yesterday count for ANYTHING??? Of course we had no one to blame but ourselves, so we accepted his harsh ruling in humble defeat, and Lawrence went ahead and took the test. Oh, you want to know if Lawrence passed the test? Well, the tester couldn't tell us yet because I'm sure there is a very complicated grading process that involves higher math skills and several hours in a locked room with no one there to disturb him. I know this because he said we can't find out until 4:30 p.m., so what else must it be?

The Kids SEEM To Be Picking Up The Language

I was so proud of my daughter, Lexi, today. She answered the phone to an apparent Hebrew-speaking caller, and had a brief Hebrew-only conversation! I didn't hear what she said but I could tell she was speaking in Hebrew. When she got off the phone I told her how proud I was. She was pleased that I was proud but looked a little surprised. I asked her what the conversation was about. She said that she answered the phone and after a brief moment she said into the phone, *"Ani lo medaberet Ivrit"* ("I don't speak Hebrew") and hung up!!

Eitan, on the other hand, seems to be getting along fine with the Hebrew speakers. He has made friends with a number of boys from his only-Hebrew-speaking bunk and has even had some afternoon playdates with them. When I ask him what he talks about with them, he answers in classic Eitan-style, "I dunno!" Except this time, I believe him!!

Our First Car-less Day

So sad, we returned the car. But car, or no car, it was a too-hot-to-stay-home day, and we were going to the museum no matter what! We quickly hiked up to the top of the hill to catch the once-an-hour bus and got there a half hour early. The bus then took 45 minutes to NOT take us to the destination we were supposed to go to. So we decided to take a cab. But we were seven people (6 of us plus a friend). So what, we thought, we can squish. So we hailed a five-passenger cab. Not like a mid-sized five passenger, this thing was a MICRO-sized. Twenty shekels, the cabby said. Anyway, we all pile on top of each other, barely get the door closed, and the cabby turns and looks at us and counts seven and told us we were too many and he couldn't take us. So we piled out and looked for a plus-sized taxi. Then we said: "Forget it, lets just take two cabs."

Our cabby was still there so we hailed him again and told him our plan. He said, "That will cost you another 20 shekels. If you're paying 40 shekels anyway I'll take all of you for the 40." We must have been really hot because apparently our brains had melted. Once we were willing to PAY for two cabs, why not RIDE in two cabs? You know what it's like for six people to squeeze into a narrow three-passenger seat, in 100 DEGREES?!?!

We went to the Israel Museum which I thought was a very new-immigrant-to-Israel thing to do. Of course my kids just thought it was a very dorky thing to do, and couldn't we just go to the mall? The boys surprised me by loving every minute of it. The girls surprised me by not being in the museum gift shop the entire time they were there. (Actually maybe it's because I didn't let them). Anyway, *I* had a good time.

Our First Package

My parents sent us a package a while ago and we'd been waiting anxiously for it. Not because it was so valuable, but because we wanted to know that a package could get to us here. The good news is, the package arrived!! Now for the bad news: Our mail delivery is only 4 days a week: Sun, Mon, Tues, and Wed. In Wednesday's delivery the notice was placed that the package is in. Problem is, by the time we got Wednesday's mail, it was too late to pick up a package – and it won't be open again until Sunday night!! At least we know where it is.

The Continuing Sagas

1. Lawrence finished putting up the living room curtains. He hates them. Actually, they are pretty bad. Too bad we bought them from so far away. They looked so nice in the package! I don't know what we'll do, but for now at least it's covered!

2. Lawrence passed his driver's test! We found out the real reason we weren't told this morning: One time, 10 years ago, a kid was told on the spot that he had failed, and he beat up the tester!

3. The Lift: So I guess you figured out it didn't come today either. They made a special arrangement to deliver it to us first thing tomorrow morning, even thought they don't work Fridays. But that didn't work out. Then I heard Sunday might not work out either. Well, whatever. The bright side is that I won't have to be unpacking all weekend. Maybe it will take them until next Thursday when we'll finally have the truck that will move the furniture off of our lawn. (Luckily we wait until the last minute and haven't yet PUT the furniture on our lawn!) We'll keep you posted!

Journal Entry #23: Sunday, August 4

Our Trip To The Mall

I made two observations today on my first outing to the Malcha Mall in Jerusalem since I've arrived. Just to acquaint you with it, it is a huge indoor mall with many stores and restaurants, similar to any mall in the U.S. but without The Gap. Anyway, so we arrived at the mall and I started turning my head in every direction like a child. I wasn't looking at the myriad of stores. I wasn't looking at the choices of restaurants (for a change!). I was looking at all of the people. Everywhere I looked I saw Jews of every "stripe". Many religious Jews, with every different kind of kippot (skullcaps) and women's head coverings, plus many non-religious; In every category there were young and old; families, girlfriends, couples. It's funny because I've been all over and certainly seen all of the above. What made this different was the fact that we were in a mall. Because this mall is in Jerusalem there happens to be a large percentage of obviously observant Jews. It's really a hard thing for me to explain, it was almost like being at a synagogue, or a special rally for a Jewish cause, except that we were all simply "at the mall". The point here is that I became so emotional over the whole thing that I started to cry. It was just one more reminder of where I am and why I am here. Because this land is MINE.

The other observation I made also had to do with the people. There were so many!! I don't think I've ever been to a mall that was that crowded. I was very pleased to see so many people out and about, living their lives, and shopping.

A Sleeping Bag Without A Zipper Just Isn't A Bag

Tonight we helped Shira with her last minute preparations for *Machaneh*, a yearly camping event for each grade under the auspices of the Bnei Akiva youth movement. She is leaving tomorrow morning at 7:30 a.m. for three days. Obviously she needed a sleeping bag for this tent-less event. As avid campers we have plenty of sleeping bags. Of course they are all tucked away in our lift on a dock somewhere. I found a neighbor with a sleeping bag, but at the last minute I couldn't reach her. At 10:45 I called a friend, desperate, and she found one. I ran up the block, grabbed it, zoomed home, and sat down to zip and fold it and put this last and very important item in her suitcase. Except, that there was no zipper. Not a broken zipper, NO zipper. Actually I have a number of sleeping bags like this one right in my house. We call them "blankets".

Today's News

For those of you who don't know, there were four terror attacks here today, with close to ten people killed and many injured. I know that for many of you your first thoughts are to us at times like these. For some of you we are the only people you know in Israel. Therefore we felt compelled to share with you some of our thoughts at this difficult time.

First of all, our strongest emotion is one of anger, as opposed to fear. Anger at the Palestinian terrorists who murder Jews for pleasure. Anger at the Palestinian people who have had opportunity after opportunity to stand up against such killings; stand up and rally for peaceful protests; Who instead have celebrations in the streets and pass out candy when Jews and Americans are killed. Anger at the U.N., E.U., and the nations of the world for not having a problem with all of this. Anger at the President of the United States who despite all that has happened, and despite the very war against terror that the U.S. is still actively engaged in, still talks about fighting this terror war in Israel through diplomacy and negotiations. (How exactly do you negotiate with someone who wants you dead?) Finally, anger at Israel for catering too much to a world that doesn't care much anyway, and not getting rid of Arafat and his terrorists once and for all.

As far as life goes here, I'll address some of the questions I've received in my answer. First of all, we don't actually hear all of the tanks and incursion stuff that you read about. We do not live anywhere near Nablus or Jenin or Tulkarm or Gaza. We do live quite close to Bethlehem and Hebron, but not close enough to see or hear anything. There are roadblocks here and there that most people just pass through. Today we saw additional roadblocks and checkpoints, but people mostly did whatever they need to do. Which I think is very important, because if you live your life with fear, then the terrorists have succeeded. We are all very alert here and watching for suspicious people and things. Unfortunately we are dealing with a culture that we don't understand. A culture where nothing is sacred in their warped desire to rid Israel of all of its Jews. A woman who did not successfully carry out a planned suicide attack was to use a real baby as part of her disguise. How do you fight against that? Our natural desire to use sympathy, empathy, HUMANITY, just doesn't work because something in their humanity is lost.

Journal Entry #24: Monday, August 5

The Lift Is Here!!!

It is quite amazing, but true. We woke up this morning expecting more of the same delays. Then, the unbelievable happened: they called to tell us the container was on its way. Nice of them to give us so much notice, but we were so happy it was finally coming that we just did what we had to. Which was basically emptying our house of some huge pieces of borrowed furniture without any help of course because we HAD NO NOTICE. Oh well. So we enlisted the kids and started emptying drawers, rolling up carpet, shlepping beds and couches. When we were done, our front lawn looked something like a messy yard sale. (What I wouldn't give for it to look that good now!) Turned out we had plenty of time so we swept and mopped. We were going to do this RIGHT. Our lift would be brought, and sorted and put away before you could blink. What a nice plan. Next time I have such a plan I'll move with a mini U-Haul. Let me just tell you that people should not be allowed to move to Israel with forty foot containers. Anyone out there planning Aliyah, don't have the shipping company tell you what size lift you need – just ask him what will fit in a twenty foot container. And don't take anything more!!

Okay, let's back up a bit. How cool is it that the very container that we watched get packed up with all our stuff in Boca Raton was now pulling up right in front of our house in Neve Daniel! Then this team of six guys came out and they were moving fast – but it was much more manageable than on the moving-out end. Lawrence or I stood at the door with the inventory list and just told them which room to put everything into. This was just fine except that by the time the container was only a quarter emptied, most of the rooms were full. This was a problem. And it didn't fit well with my plan to put everything away before you could blink. So we started to improvise a bit. Maybe put the toys in the boys room instead of the playroom. How about the linen in the living room? I knew it was getting out of control when the only place for the wardrobe was in the dining room. But it didn't really matter anymore. There was so much stuff everywhere that some rooms were wall to wall, floor to ceiling, filled with boxes.

Now the appliances, that was something else all together. First of all, you gotta see these guys moving appliances. They were oxen! One guy would put a washing machine on his back and carry it down the stairs. A washing machine! Speaking of washing machines, there is a room designed as a laundry room in this house – for midgets that is. Not only could the washing machine not fit in the door to the laundry room, but there wouldn't be room for the dryer, too, if we even got it in.

While we are on things fitting, something amazing happened on the container. Besides that our boxes had babies (since there is no other way to explain the enormous number of boxes that emerged from that container), but our furniture actually expanded. I'm not joking! We have this little couch that was going to go in the big multi-purpose room downstairs. That couch was really small. Now, it is humongous! We can't even fit it in the room!

Oh, and about that room. Our landlady has the use of that room until this Thursday for her day care. Since we ran out of spaces to put everything, they started piling stuff up in that room. (Good thing she wasn't there!) Well, remember that washing machine that didn't fit into the laundry room? Yup, and the dryer too. Squashed into that room that doesn't even fit our couch. We stayed up until 3 a.m. arranging and rearranging that room so that her little kids would have where to go. My husband even had his grand opportunity to be an ox like those moving guys when he used his back to lift up a wall unit, since the only helper he had at 2 a.m. was weak, little me.

There was one glitch last night. We were so busy dealing with the invasion of our stuff that we completely forgot about a 9:30 p.m. meeting we had with the Membership Council of our neighborhood. We had arranged this meeting, which is to determine our eligibility as permanent residents of this community, before we knew that the lift was coming today. At 9:50 p.m. they called us up wondering where we were. Bad way to start! Unfortunately our girls weren't home to babysit and the boys were sleeping. But they told us to come, so we carried our sleeping boys to a neighbor's house, and walked up to the top of the hill for this meeting. We arrived huffing and puffing, in our end-of-a-moving-day clothes, to a meeting that was conducted almost entirely in Hebrew. And we had to make a good impression! Oh well. I'll tell you about that whole process another day.

Journal Entry #25: Wednesday, August 7

The Unpacking Begins

Let me tell you something about myself: I hate unpacking. No, I mean I really hate it. I'm slow, disorganized, and never know where to put anything. This is not a good combination with the contents of a forty-foot container. We started bright and early yesterday at about 12:40 p.m. (You can tell I couldn't wait to start!) Things were going fine until Lawrence discovered a big puddle on the floor in the one room that was packed like a sardine can with boxes. This could not be a good thing. We had to empty out half the room to find the culprit. Turns out it was a refill-size bottle of liquid SoftSoap. There was just enough left in the bottle to fill a small bottle with one whole inch of soap. The rest of the soap was all over the box, its contents, the box beneath it, the floor, everything around it, and my feet. Look, it could have been worse. At least everything will be clean!

Can you imagine if it was my maple syrup that spilled? (Not to mention how upset I would have been to lose my precious maple syrup!)

Somehow My Kids Know Everyone

My sons were just picked up by a boy Eitan's age (eight) to go to some sort of bonfire, and as I watched them from the window, they walked towards three other boys who were calling out "Eitan!!" and waving. My son waved back as the neighborhood boy who was walking him asked Eitan who they were. How does my kid know more people than the ones who have been living here?

A Warm Welcome From . . . The Garbage Men

This morning Lawrence was bringing trash to the dumpster when the garbage men happened to arrive for their pick-up. It was obvious that this was no ordinary garbage pick-up since all of our boxes and bubble wrap were piled high outside the dumpster and there was Lawrence with more of it. They asked Lawrence if he had just moved in and he said we were *olim chadashim* (new immigrants). The garbage men said a warm *Bruchim Habaim* – Welcome to Israel! They asked him all sorts of questions, and wished him well. Only in Israel!

Soapy Floors Do Have Advantages

So remember the SoftSoap spill? Clean-up was quite an event. Bubble production was at an all-time high. I got the puddle cleaned up, but there was still a huge soapy residue. Lawrence wasn't in the room so I decided the heck with it, he won't notice. He noticed. He wanted to know why I didn't finish cleaning up the spill, since he needed to rearrange all of the boxes in the room. I told him it would help him slide the heavy boxes around. And you know what? It did help. So the lesson learned from all this is that if you ever need to move boxes around, first polish your floor with SoftSoap.

The State Of Our Stuff

So far, our things have been largely intact. The damage we have discovered was broken glass on two framed pictures and a broken leg on our sleeper sofa. The sofa looks lovely right now, lying on its side. Oh, and a bottle of Sabra liqueur that wasn't closed tight and, you guessed it, leaked out entirely all over whatever it was near. None of this is serious, though, and we have insurance so we will simply make a claim.

Any Car Will Do

One thing about living in Neve Daniel, you have to have a car!! And we don't of course. We plan to buy a car, but first we need our driver's licenses and I'm still serving my punishment for being late last week and haven't taken my test. Then once we get our licenses, it will take anywhere from two to six weeks depending on which car we choose. We told our friend that we were going to rent a car since we so badly needed one in the meantime. This shocked her and she said she would try to find a car for us. People here are very generous about sharing things, even cars. The trick is to find someone who just happens to have a car sitting there that they are not using. Within the next 24 hours I'll let you know if we borrowed, stole or rented.

Journal Entry #26: Thursday, August 8

Sometimes Driving Through Tunnels Here IS Scary

View Of Neve Daniel

Yesterday I was in the car with my friend on the way through Jerusalem on the "Super Express Highway" called the Begin Road. It's basically a shortcut through Jerusalem with three lanes, a long tunnel, and usually quick passage from north to south. Just before the exit that we didn't want to take, there seemed to be some sort of tie up. It appeared that all three lanes were closed but there was no one directing traffic off of the highway, so how could that be? Maybe the traffic light was broken? We watched as the various cars around us vacillated between going forward, staying put, or turning around. No joke! ON this three lane highway, there were actually a few cars that made U-turns or reversed right off of the highway! Turns out they were the SMART ones. We were part of the small group that guessed on the light being broken. We started off slowly into the tunnel. Smooth sailing! Hey, this was easy! "Ha, Ha!" to all the dummies sitting in traffic back there!

All of a sudden we heard a blaring loudspeaker. I could only understand one word: *"Mishtara"* (Police). My friend, who was driving, understood it all: "ALL OF YOU IN THE TUNNEL GO DIRECTLY TO THE POLICE!"

We were scared! We also didn't listen to instructions. Like the majority of other cars who ventured into the tunnel, we high-tailed it out of there – IN REVERSE! Meanwhile, Ezra (the only kid in the car) piped up, "This is NOT safe." We got out of the tunnel, and sat in the front of the traffic totally stuck now between the tunnel and masses of cars behind us. Within two minutes the light turned green and we passed through the tunnel legally. But we were surprised that there wasn't a cop waiting for us at the other end of the tunnel! Let me just say that it was an experience.

The Scare Of My Life

Last night Lawrence and I were working very hard trying to get the house to start looking more like a house and less like a warehouse. One after another my kids took baths and got ready for bed while we were largely uninvolved with their bedtime routine since we were so busy and it was late. At one point it was very quiet and I was thinking that everyone had gone to bed when I realized that my child, **Joe***, had never come out of the bath. Wow, that seemed like a long time. I thought I'd go check and make sure everything was okay. I knocked gently on the door. "Joe?" I called out. Joe didn't answer.

I knocked louder and called out a little more urgently, "Joe?!" Still no answer.

Maybe Joe fell asleep!, I thought in alarm. **"JOE!?!"** I screamed, and started pounding on the door.

At this point Lawrence was on high alert and came rushing up. I was screaming and screaming Joe's name and pounding as hard as I could. Why wouldn't Joe wake up? Why are these **stupid doors** impossible to unlock from the outside!?!? There was not a moment to spare. I yelled for Lawrence to break the door down. I think he was about to do it anyway. Meanwhile, I was already dialing our physician neighbor across the street, anticipating the need for CPR. One, two, three, HEAVE! The door went crashing in! Shaking with fear I rushed into the bathroom. There was my precious, beautiful child lying in the bathtub. Sleeping peacefully like a baby. With convulsive sobs I scooped up my oblivious child into the tightest hugs imaginable.

What is wrong with you, my child wanted to know. And why was I in the bathroom, during my child's bath and with the door wide open, in fact what in the world happened to the door? But nothing mattered at that point. My child was safe. Lawrence and I just hugged and cried.

*name changed to protect the privacy of the individual

Struck By A Driver's Test

Remember that "punishment" we received for being a few minutes late for our driver's test? Well this is the punishment that keeps on giving. Today, after a whole week, I got the call from my driving instructor that he had finally rescheduled my test, for Monday, August 12th. Problem is that we are leaving for Eilat on Sunday! I said that I'm sorry but that won't work, I will be away.

"You must come!" he said.

"How can I come? I already made my reservations," I replied.

Then came the kicker: "If you don't come, it is a fail," he said in his delightful English. Okay, I'll come.

Our One Month Anniversary

Yep, it is exactly one month since we last had a washing machine! (Not what you thought I'd say, huh?) The laundry has piled up so high that we have had to stuff it right into the huge duffel bags that we came in. We did have this little, microscopic, ancient, European washing machine that looks like a Chinese torture thing. We finally learned how to use it, but we don't have a dryer and it's a huge pain. So we've been washing a load here and there at various neighbors, when desperate we've been using the Chinese

Publix it isn't, but shopping is a pleasure in our makolet

torture machine, or just going without. Yesterday our dream came true. Our friends next door went away for two days and let us use their washer/dryer for the two days! We are in heaven! I mean, this is the meaning of true bliss! You think I'm crazy? YOU go for a month without doing laundry for four kids who sweat, and get dirty and go to sleep-away-camp twice. Exactly. True bliss.

3

Acclimating...

Journal Entry #27: Saturday, August 10

Our First Shabbos At Home

The first of everything is very special. The first Shabbos at home was especially so. Since we arrived in Neve Daniel, we have been invited out for all of the Shabbos meals and some others. While this has made it much easier for us, we badly needed a breather, and my kids were getting quite tired of falling asleep in people's homes since the Friday night meal could go on forever. It wasn't quite so simple since we had neither a table nor the pots/pans/silverware to do it with. That's not exactly true. We had all the stuff since Monday, but it was buried in mountains of boxes, and the table had been dismantled and wrapped and needed to be put back together. But we were determined, and we began an all-out quest to find everything we needed. We were almost completely successful, except for my food processor, so we did without potato kugel.

So Friday progressed with the smells of Shabbos getting stronger, as my chicken soup bubbled on the stove, and brownies (Duncan Hines) baked in the oven. All that was left was the table. Lawrence cleared a space for it in the dining room, dragged the whole, heavy wrapped package inside, and opened it. There was the tabletop. But where in the world were the legs? All along we had assumed that the legs and table were packaged together. Wouldn't that be a bright idea. No legs. We started looking furiously through all of the boxes to try to find those darn legs. No legs. Now it was almost Shabbos and we had no table to eat on. Luckily we remembered the folding table that we had bought (and were able to find!) – so out came the folding table, and we had a lovely Shabbos meal on it.

By the way, three out of four of our kids were asleep before the meal was over, and we truly appreciated not having to carry anyone back!

Driver's License Test: Next Stage

You know, it's good to know the right people. Our next-door-neighbor and very good friend is a lawyer. One hour before Shabbat we called him and told him our tale of woe, that the driving instructor guy wasn't letting us go on our trip to Eilat. What kind of nonsense is this, he immediately wanted to know. You call him and tell him you can't make it, and he'll just have to reschedule you. I explained to him that I said all that and I was told under no uncertain terms that I either take the test on Monday or I fail. I asked him if he could please use his persuasive words, not to mention his fluent Hebrew, and see what he could do. Despite the lateness of the hour (almost Shabbos) he agreed to make the call. Did I ever need him! Even with all of the above, it was no short, sweet, easy phone call. He ended the call leaving the ball in his court, telling him to reschedule my test and call me with the new date. Let's see what happens!

Journal Entry #28: Sunday, August 11

A Trip Without A Camera

We started our day with a *tiyul* (trip) around Gush Etzion. The trip was designed for the new immigrant families, to show us the beauty and history of the land we now call home. And, yes, I forgot my camera. And believe me, there were NO Seven-Elevens on the road to get a disposable one! Mountains, sheep, and donkeys, but no Seven-Elevens.

Something In Israel That Caused Me Real Fear

Speaking of sheep, one of the stops we made was at a little settlement that raises sheep. We all offloaded the bus and trekked down to where the sheep were hanging out in pens. The kids especially enjoyed both the little lambs, and the big males who had the huge horns that the kids recognized as what a *shofar* is made from.

So what was I afraid of? Well you see there were these three dogs hanging out with the sheep. All of a sudden, two of the dogs each decided that the other must die. I mean these dogs were out for blood! Imagine this: There are all these families including MY CHILDREN, and about 30 sheep in a little pen with these psycho dogs blocking their only way out, and me on the other side of them with Eitan, watching this horrible event unfold and praying that neither dog will decide to attack one of the children instead. Their owner was trying desperately to get them off of each other, and I wondered how much more effective he would be if it was a child the dogs were attacking instead. People have asked me many times if I was afraid since moving to Israel. OK, folks. I was afraid!

The end of the story, by the way, is the dogs were finally pulled apart and separated, nobody was mauled, and I couldn't wait to get out of there.

The Effects Of My Journal

During this Gush Etzion tiyul, which, you may remember, was directly preceding our five-day trip to Eilat, we received a phone call from a friend. Were we in fact going to Eilat today, they wanted to know, because they were looking to take a vacation. How in the world did you know we were going to Eilat? I asked. The journal! They were of the small but growing group of people in Israel who receive it.

"Yes we're going, we're leaving in two hours, and we'd love for you to join us," we told them.

How they did it, we don't know but they were at our house before we even loaded the car. Driving so far with another family is much more fun than alone. Especially when you can swap a kid or two and break up all the sibling rivalry issues, which we did.

The Drive

If you've never taken the drive down to Eilat in Israel, you must do it even if you have no desire to go there (which I can understand). The drive was unbelievable. About halfway down we stopped at the huge crater in Mitzpe Ramon. Crater? This was a Grand Canyon! Also called a *machtesh,*

Mitzpe Ramon – The Grand Canyon of Israel

it is a unique and spectacular geological phenomenon. And in true, Israeli, let-everyone-fend-for-themselves style, there was absolutely no fence, gate, guardrail, or even a rope along the whole edge of an incredibly steep, tall, rocky cliff. But gorgeous! It was worth pretending that I'm not afraid of heights for those few minutes.

When we were done up there, we went back in the car where the road took us right down and into the canyon! Beautiful! There were multicolored layers of rock that were clearly visible all along the sides of the craters inner rim, but what was more amazing was the multicolored sands that were everywhere. I think I will collect some on the way back. There was aqua, and purple, and pink, and all shades of brown and tan – and this went on for a while!

As we went along driving deeper and deeper into the desert, the land became more barren. What a dumb word! There may have been nothing growing, but "barren" just doesn't describe it. And who said there was nothing growing, anyway? We'd be driving along the desert when all of a sudden there would be a village with green grass and palm trees. Or an enormous grove of date palms.

I love this land. Driving through it and going from mountains to farmland to desert to beach – in one afternoon! It's unbelievable! It is truly an ever changing landscape and I love every part of it! Eilat, on the other hand...

About Eilat

We've just arrived in a strange and foreign land called Eilat. I think it is a distant cousin to South Beach in Miami, Florida, with a little bit of Vegas and Hell sprinkled in. Hell, by the way, is not because of the easy entry pass one could acquire to there while in Eilat, but because of the HEAT! Did you ever stand in front of a car exhaust and get that heat blown on you? That's Eilat. Weather-wise, anyway. As far as the rest, well let me tell you. Our other friends arrived earlier today. They called to warn us that the hotel lobby was like a bus station in the part of town we wouldn't go to. People were wearing very little clothes, but body piercing and tattoos were in abundance. Not your typical family vacation spot!

When we arrived it was hard to believe we were still in Israel. A beautiful row of hotels were lighting up the summer night sky. Neon lights were everywhere! Stores, shops, restaurants, it was so bright! And the people – well let's just say that at least we were not surprised.

After settling into our room, we took in one boardwalk attraction, Trampolining. I made an amazing discovery while we were there: I do not have as much stamina as I did when I was a kid.

Journal Entry #29: Monday, August 12

What an amazing day!! We started out by going to the Underwater Observatory Marine Park here in Eilat. The view from there was spectacular. Actually, where is the view not spectacular? Luckily I DID have my camera this time and I utilized it in abundance. That was fun. But the fun was only just beginning!

The Yacht

We reserved a turn-of-the-century (last century, not this century) schooner for a private three-hour cruise. (We were five families). But that wasn't enough. Maybe we could do water sports off of the boat. And we could! Banana boat? Sure. Snorkeling? Why not? Parasailing? Definitely!! So like a bunch of spoiled dummies we added all of these things to our cruise. We set sail about 5:20 p.m. We were 10 adults and close to 20 kids. Right away the kids took over the boat. They were in heaven! And so were we. The kids were very well behaved and the yacht was charming. All polished wood and beautifully kept; the younger boys felt like we were on a pirate's ship.

Playing in Eilat

Banana Boating

Unfortunately the timing didn't work out very well. Then again, how could it when you try to cram so many things into one excursion? Anyway, the parasail boat came and took the first eight brave ones, and shortly after the boat pulling the banana boat arrived. Ezra and I went along with my two friends and four others onto the boat. Ezra, as the eighth passenger, had no intention of actually riding the banana boat, but as long as he was one of the eight, he could remain in the motorboat. So the seven of us climbed onto this long, inflated banana-thing, each with our own handle to hold onto. Then, the boat sped away! And we were speeding right along behind it! What fun!! You really had to hold on; we had wind and a nearly-constant salt-water spray in our face. It was such a thrill! We had a stunning view of the big hotels, the mountains, the Gulf of Akaba, and Ezra on the boat. And there we were, out on the Red Sea. It was just incredible!

Parasailing

Immediately on our return from the banana-boating, they ushered the eight of us onto the parasail boat. It all happened so fast, and I still had Ezra (he's five!) – so there we were on this parasail boat, getting instructions, when I asked for the heck of it if Ezra was too young to do it, and they said he could ride with me. Great idea! As dumb as this sounds, I was much more nervous about going alone. What HE could have done to save me, I have no idea. Actually it turned out that I became more nervous thinking about what I could do to save HIM if I'd need to. Anyway, he agreed to go and we got harnessed up. Let me tell you that something scary is much scarier when you are a mother and your child is experiencing the same scary thing. There we were 60 meters (that's METERS, not feet) up in the air, dangling by some ratty parachute, and there was NOTHING I could do to protect my kid. All of my maternal instincts were completely wasted up there. But what a thrill! They do this "tea-bag dunking" thing where they slowly let you drop until you're actually in the water and then lift you up again. I was a little scared and so was Ezra, but we really enjoyed it after all and we're glad we went. Ezra wants to do it again!

Snorkeling

Oh yeah, about the snorkeling. There was no snorkeling. It's not that we didn't have the equipment, but there just wasn't any time! In fact, some of the people didn't even get to go parasailing! (Much to their chagrin, but that's another story altogether, and they're getting to go tomorrow). They did do some swimming off the boat, and even got to swing from this "Tarzan" rope into the water. Of course I didn't see any of it because I was sailing in the sky at the time.

Anyway, the whole experience was amazing. We had so much fun!

Back To The Hotel

Talk about tired!! We were wiped out by the time we got back. My friend and I were with all our kids when we finally got back to the hotel and arrived at the elevator. Seeing all our kids start to cram into the elevator, we decided to just plop down on the bench 10 feet away and take the next elevator. So we plopped down on the bench and watched as the elevator door closed and took our kids upstairs. Then it occurred to us: there is absolutely NO WAY to get that elevator back down without one of us getting up and pressing the button. You see, elevators don't run like buses on a schedule even if you badly want them to.

Journal Entry #30: Tuesday, August 13

Our Great Camel Adventure

Our day started out with the family split up: Lawrence, Lexi and Eitan went to get the few parasail rides that were owed to us from yesterday. In the end, all six of us had gone up! I'm not sure what Shira did, but I took Ezra and joined our friends on a camel safari. We got to this really old, middle-eastern looking place – like stepping back in time at least 100 years if not five hundred more. They had this whole caravan of camels ready to go, and we loaded up on them. We felt like we were doing the real thing until we realized that there was no camel for the guide. What in the world is he going to ride on, we wondered. The safari began with him leading our caravan out of the enclosed area of the center and into the open mountains. Were we about to climb those steep mountain paths, we wondered? More importantly, what was our guide going to ride? All too quickly we realized that the guide would not be riding after all. He was to lead our caravan on foot. This was quite disappointing since it would obviously hamper our speed, and the terrain we could cover.

My friend behind me, with a baby in her lap on the camel, questioned, "Why is this bad? We can't go fast anyway!"

"You're right," I assured her, "but if he were on a camel too, I wouldn't KNOW if we were going fast or slow, even if it were the same exact pace. But if he's walking the camels, it's like an extra-long pony ride."

Despite my unfulfilled desire to gallop the camels, it was quite enjoyable. The trip was capped off with a little siesta on cushions under a canopy where our guide made us sweet tea and fresh laffa bread while we sat there being served.

Swimming In An Aquarium

I think I did just that today. The aquarium is called the Red Sea. We drove south of our hotel, almost to the border with Egypt (Sinai), which is actually only several kilometers from where we are staying. We set up shop on the beach with all of our stuff, including quite a bit of snorkeling equipment. I have never gone snorkeling. In fact, I don't think I've ever gone swimming in salt water. (I've been in it many times, but never done

Snorkeling - Just beautiful!

face-in swimming). I watched as many others put masks on and viewed the incredible underwater sights. They told me it was incredible, but I hadn't seen it for myself. Finally I decided I would just do it. Lawrence told me what to do and I did it! WOW! It was an unbelievable experience!! It was like a big secret that everyone knew about and I was let in on it today. There were beautiful fish of all sizes swimming right around us!! It feels like you're flying. When you're just swimming, you go UNDER water. When you are snorkeling, you are ABOVE everything else that is under water! Do you understand the difference? It was incredible. And doing such a special thing with my husband was just a beautiful experience.

Journal Entry #31: Saturday, August 17

Enemy Kites Flying Overhead?

On our way back from Eilat, we drove the last few miles on a road we had never been on. It happened to go right through an Arab village. As we were driving I noticed two kites overhead. It struck me at that moment that there are Arab children who romp and play like any others. I saw some children sitting on their porch watching us. Any place in the Western world those same kids might be on a Little League team with my sons. Or perhaps we would have found ourselves flying a kite at a park with those kite flyers.

Please realize, though, that this is not the Western world. Although Israel is a democracy in its government, there is no Martin Luther Abdullah Jr. staging peace marches and preaching for civil rights. If only one strong

Arab would even bother to galvanize his people and make an effort towards real peace, maybe there would be a chance. This is not what our reality is though. I will be frank with you – please don't get nervous because knowing or not knowing the facts does not change them in any way: there is a death warrant out on Jews in Israel. That is right. A death warrant. What does this mean exactly? It means that Arabs have what they consider to be a "nationalistic" justification to kill ME. It means that my sons will not be playing in Little League with an Arab's son. It means that we won't be flying any kites in their parks, and, hopefully, they won't be flying any in ours.

Don't feel so bad for us. The death warrant is on all of you too. Everyone who receives this directly from me is either Jewish, American or both. That puts you on the list. Does this mean that there are no Arabs who are good citizens, would not hurt a fly, and want nothing to do with all of this craziness? No, it doesn't mean that at all. I hope and pray that there are many. And all of those people deserve peace and all of the blessings I would wish on anyone else. But how do I know that they are there, if they don't stand up for what they believe in? Are the Arabs incapable of producing a King, Jr.? A Gandhi? Where are all those peace lovers that the U.N. and the E.U. want us to make peace with? Why won't they make themselves heard? How are we to know the difference between those that support the death warrant and those that don't? To be quite honest, I wouldn't recommend Little League with them any time soon. It is difficult to play ball with someone who wants you dead.

Cliffhangers

I see that my journalistic abilities are leaving much to be desired as I have been leaving cliffhangers and then forgetting about them.

#1- How did we get to Eilat? I had mentioned that my friend was shocked that we would have to RENT a car. She came through! Actually, the other family that we were going with lent us their second car on our friend's suggestion.

#2- The Driver's License. Well, this one is still a cliffhanger. Last you all heard my friend had called the driving instructor who had scheduled my test to tell him he must reschedule. I called him on Sunday – on the way down to Eilat – and I received the great news that I could reschedule the test. Yay!! I've now gone through my calendar and told him exactly which days I am not available and he will reschedule my test accordingly (let's hope!). Of course then there's the hurdle of passing the test. Hopefully my 17 years of driving experience will help there. Too bad very few of those years were with a stick shift car!

Let's Talk About The Weather...

Seriously – the weather is actually quite interesting here. We spent a week in Eilat where the average daily temperature was OVER 100 degrees, lows somewhere in the 80s. No joke! Every single day!! Then drove a Boca Raton-to-Orlando-distance and arrived in a low 80s. for a high (if it even got that warm) with a strong breeze, nighttime temps around 60 with wind! (And it's still over 100 in Eilat)

Journal Entry #32: Tuesday, August 20

More Punishment...

...this time from the appliance service guy. Of course we had no washing machine or dryer until our lift arrived. This was quite irritating to say the least. Six people wear a lot of clothes and make a lot of laundry. But, what can you do? The lift was coming when it was coming, and the washer and dryer were coming with it. So we tolerated it. Then – it came!! Our brand new, shiny appliances were brought into our house. I was never so excited to do laundry before!! I immediately called the company that's contracted to set up the appliances, to have them come out right away. This was on Monday, August 5th. "Sorry," they said, "but we won't be in your area until next week."

"Next week!" I said in alarm, "but we will be away next week! Couldn't you possibly do it this week?"

"Impossible," they said. They told us they would let us know early next week.

We shlepped bushels of laundry to our friends' homes and waited. They finally set our appointment for Thursday, August 15 – already outrageously late for an August 5th arrival. The problem was that we certainly would not be home from Eilat in time. So we gave our key to a neighbor in desperation and hoped all would work out with taking apart the washing machine to fit it through the door, knocking out a panel of window for the dryer vent, and whatever else.

So, we went to Eilat. While we were there the subject of the serviceman kept coming up. Lawrence was so concerned about the huge amount that needed to be done to make it right, and how could we have them do that while we were not there? I, however, was so concerned about the huge amount of LAUNDRY that needed to be done, and WHO CARES if they do it right. But our friends all agreed with Lawrence so we reluctantly called to change our appointment.

Now, for the punishment. It is now a week from the day we cancelled and we not only don't have use of our washer/dryer yet, we don't even have an appointment! We called again today to demand the service we require. In fact I called personally and did the screaming-housewife-with-mountains-of-laundry-and-now-my-children-have-lice-and-I-have-to-wash-everything-bit. (It's true!! Do you feel bad for us? He didn't.) I actually begged him and told him I would do ANYTHING if he would please come and set up our washer/dryer. This was his answer: "We almost cancelled everyone in Gush Etzion that day, because you cancelled. I don't know when we'll be back in Neve Daniel."

So now we're being punished. We *almost* messed up his whole Thursday, so they might never come and take care of us. What is so unbearably frustrating is that Lawrence is fully capable of the entire installation process, but doing that would void the warranty. By the way, the dude at the service company is completely aware of Lawrence's ability, and additionally he can authorize Lawrence to do it (or at least he can have him do it unofficially and sign off on it himself). But NO! We have to be punished because we almost messed up his Thursday.

...But We Still Have Smiles!

Today we were mostly home trying to get through a seemingly never-ending supply of packed boxes. In the middle of everything Lawrence and the kids took a spontaneous break and were outside tossing a football around. Everyone had a huge smile on his/her face and it put a big smile on mine as well.

What a team!

Journal Entry #33: Saturday, August 24

This One Will Blow You Away...

Neve Daniel is known for a few things: It's on a fairly high mountain so it has a spectacular view – when it's not too foggy anyway. It is also known for its wind.

Now the holiday of Sukkot is coming up, and we need to build a sukka (a kind of temporary hut that remains up for eight days in the early Fall).

These sukkot are built differently depending upon where you live and what the weather is like at that time of the year. For instance in Florida, lattice panels are often used for ventilation as it is quite hot there in the early Fall. In New York more solid materials such as plywood or canvas are used, which are somewhat more insulating against the cold. Now we are in Neve Daniel, and I thought we should ask people here what the customary materials are for sukkot in this area. The answer I got? "Whatever you use, make sure each piece has your name on it in case it blows away!"

Bright Idea?

Our next-door neighbors are doing an addition to their house. As we walked past, my husband pointed out a strange looking structure made by 2x4 beams nailed together vertically into a little hut. The door is a piece of cardboard from a shipping box sent to a different neighbor. In other words, our neighbors have their name in bold letters on the "door" of a workers' outhouse. Quite an interesting little hut they have there. Actually, it seems to be holding up to the Neve Daniel wind. Perhaps we can use their outhouse as a model for our sukkah??

Our First Dinner Party

Our good friends catered a party on Thursday night. They couldn't have it at their home so after some plan shuffling we offered them our house. The easiest way to have a party is have it be someone else's party, and have even a different person cater it. Not that we didn't do anything. But it is really great to have a party at your own home that you can be a guest at! Anyway, our friend is an incredible caterer and the affair was beautiful. If you're ever in Israel and need an affair catered, I've got the caterer for you!

Busy Week Ahead

This week all of the kids start school (yay!) We have back-to-school meetings and such for each of them. We also have a finish-the-leftovers-from-Thursday's-party BBQ tomorrow night. Just a little something with, oh, thirty-some-odd people. I may have my driver's test too. That is, if the guy ever calls me back! But most importantly, my washer and dryer are scheduled to be hooked up on Monday!!!!!! This means that the bulk of my work this week will be LAUNDRY! And I will be so happy to do that laundry!!!

Mental Check-up

We "know" that we are physically healthy since the driver's license doctor dude checked us. Once we decided we wanted to stay here in Neve Daniel, the next step was a check-up as well. An all-day battery of psychometric testing. This is a fairly routine procedure for small communities since they want to make sure no psychos or wackos move into a little neighborhood and upset things. (Any neighbors of yours come to mind who you wish had to undergo a test before moving in?) On Wednesday, Lawrence and I went to Jerusalem for that test. The first series was kind of like the Achievement tests you take in elementary school; multiple choice, several subjects, and a "do not turn the page until the instructor says so" sign at the end of each section. Anyway, we knew we were in trouble when the instructor was giving us instructions and Lawrence and I both got one of the sample questions wrong!! The next phase was how we work in a group setting. So they placed us in a room with six others and gave us scenarios to work out amongst ourselves for an hour or so. But the other six all spoke Hebrew! Next was an interview and then some essays. Luckily for me I write VERY fast. I finished my essays really quickly, then went shopping in Jerusalem while I waited for Lawrence. I had no complaints!

Journal Entry #34: Wednesday, August 28

A First Time For A Lot Of Things

Yesterday all four kids had their first day of school. How was it? Well, none of them came home crying that they want to go back to Florida, so I'll accept that as a good start. (I know that some of you may think otherwise!) Seriously, though, they all have English speakers in their classes, they all came home with something positive to say, and I didn't have to force anyone onto their school buses this morning.

I had a first yesterday as well. I accompanied Eitan to school, saw him to his classroom, then left. I started walking in the direction that Lawrence would be driving to get me. I walked alongside a beautiful, lush vineyard to my right and a grazing field to my left. There were three Arab children with some sheep on the field. As I let my gaze wander I noticed one of the children pick up what looked like a rock and throw it in what looked like my direction. This could not be. After all, these were friendly Arabs. Stunned, I looked towards them, and sure enough, they were picking up more rocks and throwing them in my direction! They were also saying something loudly in Arabic. I did not understand a word, but I assume they were not complimenting the color of my dress. They were not close enough to hit me with the rocks. Nonetheless, I would say those kids could use a good thrashing. I would be wrong, of course. It is the parents and the society they live in that could use the thrashing. A society that prides itself in poisoning children's minds is not worth anything in my book.

Now We're REALLY In The Doghouse

After the kids were all off to school, we were off shopping. For a dog. YES! We have finally decided it is time for a dog! We met with this guy who volunteers for the ASPCA and helps to find homes for dogs. He brought us to this Doggy Pension where he was housing, at his own expense, a very sweet dog who he saved from the kennel. It is a German Pointer, or, more specifically, a Poodle Pointer. A chocolate-brown, medium-sized dog with a beard and mustache like a schnauzer. Her name is "Teeka". Anyway, it wasn't instant love but she was very sweet and seemed to have the disposition we were looking for. We decided to look some more and accompany this guy to the kennel. Big mistake; for me, anyway. It's a very nice kennel for the dogs, but not for me! There were lots of dogs behind low fences that they could easily jump (and did) and other dogs attached to long chains around the perimeter of the courtyard we were walking in. Quite honestly, I was petrified! I was clinging to Lawrence and begging him to just leave already. The dogs were so loud and there were so many wandering around and coming to me, and barking. I was truly on the verge of panic. They would show us a dog and I just asked if we could please leave and just go get Teeka. Finally, we did just that. We left, and we got Teeka! We were very excited to bring her to the kids. The kids were very surprised. Now we have a dog.

Journal Entry #35: Monday, September 2

Wow, it's been a long time since I've even checked my e-mail, let alone write a journal entry. We have entered the next phase of our new and incredible Aliyah experience.

School For The Kids...

My kids have completed their first week of school. Life is very different now! Suddenly we have to wake up at 6:10 a.m. every day including Sunday! I think I need to change my clocks forward an hour or two so maybe I can trick myself into thinking I'm keeping the hours I prefer! Anyway, school has been great so far. The kids all go to school by bus. Not on a yellow school bus like in the States, but on a big tour-bus. It's so cute to see little Ezra with his little yellow backpack climbing onto this big bus. The girls have a lot of English-speakers in their class, so they have been able to make friends and feel comfortable. Eitan has a very small class so he is able to get a lot of individual attention in class. The three of them are all in English class for English speakers so that they are able to maintain their level of English reading and writing. Ezra is in a class of more Hebrew speakers, but there are a few who speak English and the teachers make an effort to speak to him in English. In any event he is happy and comes home every day with a smile on his face, so I am thrilled.

...But They're Not The Only Ones!

This week my husband and I start our Ulpan class. Ulpan is an intensive Hebrew class that is generally a five-day-a-week class that is about 5 ½ hours per day, and lasts for five months. My class started yesterday and Lawrence's starts one day this week. I was delighted to find out that my class is actually only three months long. I'm not sure why I'm delighted though. Does this mean that I will learn five months-worth of Hebrew in only three months? I'm sure the Ulpan subsidy will not continue past the three months. But at least I will feel ready to enter the workforce and start earning my millions after the three months. (Millions of what, I don't know.)

For anyone who is planning on making Aliyah, I will give you some advice: start learning Hebrew!

Oh, you think you know Hebrew already? Could you understand the news on the radio in Hebrew? Read a Hebrew novel? How about going to a lecture? Better yet, could you GIVE a lecture in Hebrew? If you answered that in the affirmative, then yes, you can ignore my advice. Otherwise, you have everything to gain by practicing reading, listening and speaking. I studied in small measures over about a year+. Really small measures. And you know what? It actually helped! Out of 6 possible levels of Ulpan, with 6 being the highest, I was placed in a 4-5 class. I love it! We're learning how to listen to the news, reading comprehension, even songs. The class is very friendly, and comprised mostly of people in the same boat as me. The class is taught entirely in Hebrew, and we are only allowed to answer in Hebrew. However, as soon as we break, the room turns into a New York-English-speaking classroom. Truly, a lot of New Yorkers! Of course I still consider myself a New Yorker too, even though I've lived in Florida for nine years.

Something strange happened when I moved to Israel. For nine years when people asked where I was from I'd say Boca Raton, FL. Now that I don't live there, my automatic answer is New York. I suppose you can take the New Yorker out of New York, but you can never take New York out of the New Yorker. But I digress.... Anyway, we have homework and everything.

Lots of memorizing too.

When I arrived home today, Lawrence was with this new French couple who'd just moved in. All I could think of was that I should have them teach me French. Of course then I gave myself a mental smack in the face and thought to myself, Could you work on one thing at a time, for once!? At least only one language!!!!! Naturally I agreed with myself, so for now my focus is Hebrew.

What About My Driver's License??

Yes, I know, it's the big question. Unfortunately the big answer is still "No." I am still waiting for the dude to set up an exam time. At least I have been getting practice on a stick-shift rental car. Now it feels like the olden days when I was in high school and could actually drive the thing. Maybe my delayed test was a blessing in disguise!!

Journal Entry #36: Thursday, September 5

A Song Of Hope?

What a neat day! It all started at my Ulpan class...

Today, being the last day of Ulpan before Rosh Hashana, we finished off the day with a party for all of the classes together. Before the party, our class was practicing some songs for Rosh Hashana. Although this is a Hebrew class, in Israel, anyone at all can take the class. As I've mentioned, this is a predominantly "New Yorker" class. However there are also three French people, two Brits, one Russian, a transvestite (I mean it!), and an Arab. Why would an Arab be taking a Hebrew class? Don't forget, they live here too. Their schools are basically taught in Arabic, and if they go on to an Israeli university, they need to know Hebrew. Anyway, we were learning a very Israeli, patriotic-type song. After we finished learning it the teacher had the whole class sing it together. During the song I stole a glance at my Arab classmate. Sure enough, he was not singing at all – just as I had expected. A few moments later I checked again, and – astonishment! – he was singing!! I checked again, and, yup! Still singing! Maybe he just loves to sing. Or maybe his Hebrew is just so bad that he had no idea what he was saying. In any case, I was impressed.

Back to our pre-Rosh Hashana party: All of the classes got together in a big room for some music and singing. Some of the classes had presentations of sorts for the others. My husband's class – minus my husband (stage fright?) – got up to do some very Jewish "Shana Tova" (Happy New Year) song. The two Arab guys in his class got up right along with them and sang.

My Favorite Drink

It's not just coffee. It's REALLY GOOD coffee. For years my day has started with a shot of perfect espresso from my Nespresso coffee machine that I received from my aunt years ago. Needless to say my 110-volt coffee machine stayed behind in 110-volt America and I was left to find a new way to make coffee in the 220-volt world. I tried a French press (decent, but depended a lot on coffee quality, and is a pain to clean), manual drip (fine in a pinch, but not a great daily option), and instant (blech!). I was lamenting recently to my aunt, since I knew that she would really understand, since she starts her day with the same coffee that I missed so much.

OK, back to my Ulpan. We were in class today when my husband received a call on his cell phone. Someone had a package for us and could they deliver it today? Sure, Lawrence told him, but what is it? They wouldn't say. But could they deliver it to us at our Ulpan? So we gave them directions to our Ulpan, and sure enough, we walked out and there was a delivery van for (drum roll, please) our favorite coffee machine! Yup, they have distributors right here in Israel. My aunt simply contacted the Israeli dealer, purchased our wonderful gift, and arranged for delivery. You thought I was happy before? Now I'm really happy!

Are They Boys Or Are They Men?

After Ulpan we went to Ben Yehudah Street at the center of town to get a book Lawrence needed for school. We were in an area where there are lots of cafes and we passed three "little boys" licking ice cream cones. Except that these boys were Israeli soldiers in full uniform carrying M-16's. Kids grow up fast here!

Back To Ben Yehudah

When I was in school here for my first year of college (seminary, really) the "in place" to go was Ben Yehudah Street; Especially on Thursday and Saturday nights. (Naturally, on those nights I could always be found there but that is another story entirely!!) Anyway, after a few bomb attacks on that street in recent years, the area turned into a ghost town and shops began closing down. In an effort to revitalize the area, they somehow created guarded entrances at every alley and street that leads to the area, and invited all sorts of artists, entertainers and food vendors to come down on Thursdays and Saturdays (and maybe other days?) to draw back the crowds. We decided to bring the family there tonight and see what it's all about. It was wonderful! There were dancers, a magician, a Jazz-Klezmer band (our favorite), all types of food, it was decorated, and best of all, there were crowds! It was so sad back in May to walk along the empty streets and see the lonely shopkeepers. Tonight there were tons of people, smiling, laughing, and having a great time. In fact, when we were watching the jazz band, a group of Israelis spontaneously broke into dance and it was such a joy to be there watching it all!

Close Encounter With A Stranger

Along with the crowds there are always the needy that collect money, either for themselves or for some organization. A deaf woman came over, asking for money for something for deaf people. She was asking for 10 shekels. I gave her five. A friend had suggested that when you give, even if you can't give much or even if you have nothing at all to give, give it with a smile, a kind word, and it's worth more than the few coins you give. With this fresh in my mind, and knowing she's deaf and even if she reads lips it's probably only in Hebrew, I gave her the five shekels with the biggest smile I had. She was so thrilled! She showed me the entire Aleph-Bet in sign language, then gave me a big hug and a kiss! I guess my friend was right.

Rosh Hashana is tomorrow. It is our New Year and a time that we traditionally send good wishes to all of our friends and loved ones. I would therefore like to sincerely wish to all of you a year of health and happiness, prosperity, and, most of all, peace.

Journal Entry #37: Thursday, September 12

STRESSSSS!!!!

This was my afternoon, so I could think of no more apt a title. Remember my driver's license test?? It was finally rescheduled for today, at 1:45 p.m. The instructor (not the tester, but the guy who gave me the lessons and whose car I was to use for the test) asked me to meet him at the testing site at 1:30-1:35 to make absolutely certain I would not be late.

1:00 – I arrive home from Ulpan, take 10 minutes to have lunch since I have plenty of time, and do not function well without my food. Have Lawrence repeat directions to the license testing place since it is in a weird spot that I can never seem to find.

1:15 – Okay, now I'm on my way to Talpiot in Jerusalem for the test. Of course there is absolutely no gas in my car and I am petrified that I won't make it to the test.

1:29 – I am approaching the gas station that is around the corner from the testing place. I might as well get gas to ease my mind, and finalize directions while I'm at it just in case.

1:34 – I leave the gas station confident with my specific directions. Left at the second light, then it will be on the left. Easy enough. How could I miss?

1:36 – I missed. Where is the testing place? I know it's very close to the gas station. But there is nothing on the left! There are no turns off the road, and no place to make a U-turn. The road continues on and I make a frantic call to Lawrence. Mind you I am driving a stick-shift car, and you're not even allowed to use a cell phone while you're driving in Israel.

1:38 – Where am I?!? Lawrence doesn't have a clue but he's trying to encourage me anyway. I throw the cell phone into my lap and make a crazy U-turn when I finally can.

1:40 – Another call is trying to come through. It's Avi the driving teacher! I disconnect with Lawrence and beg Avi for help. Avi screams into the phone (this is how he talks), "Where are you?!?"

"I don't know where I am!" I replied close to tears, "What should I do?"

1:45 – "Go left! Go right! What do you see now?!" Avi barks at me. I try to explain to him where I am. He tells me to make a left turn when I am in the right lane. I cross over all sorts of traffic to follow his instructions but to no avail. I cannot find the darn place. If the tester would see me now he would fail me before I even begin! If I don't get there immediately he *may* fail me before I begin!!

1:50 – Okay, it is really panic time now. Avi is screaming all sorts of unintelligible instructions to me in half-Hebrew and half-English. "Where are you?!?" he asks me again in total frustration.

"I'm right here!!" I am tempted to say, but I don't. At this point the tears have come and I am ready to give up the whole thing and go home.

1:53 – Breakthrough!! I realize the mistake I had been making all along. When the guy at the gas station told me to make a left at the second light, he didn't indicate that the left was a left-with-a-veer-to-the-right-and-a-quick-veer-to-the-left type of left. I see Avi waving at me from down the street. Break out the band, why don't we! Laura has finally arrived for her driving test! I wave back and pull into the parking lot. I immediately ask Avi for a glass of scotch which he seems willing to procure for me. (I decline.) I have a few minutes to wait since the tester took someone else out in the interim.

2:03 – Off I go with the tester in Avi's car. I have a lovely start wherein I am about to go the wrong way down a one way lane. And this is still in the testing parking lot!

2:05 – He has me drive on these awful, traffic-ridden streets. Oh, and someone forgot to tell me that in Israel the driving testers EXPECT you to be aggressive. Weird? I know this because when he wants me to turn left onto a busy street I wait until both sides are clear. He says, "What, you will wait all day? Cross to the middle!"

Stunned, I ask him if this is allowed. He retorts, "During your test you ask your teacher what is allowed?!"

2:08 – That's it. I certainly failed. I'll just go through the ropes of this miserable exam. I follow his instructions and keep my mouth tightly shut.

2:15 – I arrive back at the driving test place. I return the car to Avi. The first thing out of his mouth is, "Why did you try to go the wrong way down a one way lane? I hope he still passes you. If you pass I will call you this afternoon. If you fail, well, you will have to call me." So much for encouragement. (Gutless wimp!).

2:25 – I'm traveling home now a little dejected. Okay, okay – I'm bawling my eyes out. Why did I have to be so dumb?!? Well, it's not the worst thing. If I fail the test I only have to take 28 lessons before taking the next test (This is truly the law). 28 lessons? Forget it. If I fail, Lawrence will simply have to do all the driving.

2:45 – I'm home and I don't want to talk to anyone. "Don't worry, I'm sure you passed," Lawrence tries to console me.

"You don't understand," I tell him. "It was awful!"

3:45 – I am trying to busy myself with things around the house to take my mind off of it. The phone rings. I answer it. It's Avi. "Mazel Tov!" he announces. "YOU PASSED!"

Journal Entry #38: Sunday, September 15

A New Bedroom At A Price

This is not really new news, just that I haven't gotten around to mentioning it. Last week Lawrence and I played hooky from school (Ulpan) one day to go shopping. We bought our first bedroom set after fourteen years! We were quite glad that we had left this purchase until after we got here, because no American bedroom set would have fit into our bedroom. It is actually very pretty, a cherry wood (veneer, I'm sure) and it comes with the most microscopic little end tables you've ever seen. We have now moved into the downstairs bedroom that until last week had stored so many boxes that I can't imagine where we put them all. There are two problems with this "new" bedroom. The first problem is that in losing the height, we have lost our magnificent view. It has been replaced by a lovely view of our backyard – which we realize that Teeka has mistaken for her personal toilet. In other words, we went from having a view of majestic hills, and magnificent sunrises, to a view of doggy poop.

Oh, and about Teeka, she is a very nice dog but, alas, my children are not in love with her and it is not fair to them or to her for that matter, to keep her. We are looking for a new home for her.

(Any takers?)

Our Trip To Ikea

If you've never gone there, you must go. It is so much fun! I assume the one in Newark, New Jersey is similar to the one here. We borrowed a huge van and made the drive to Netanya on Tuesday evening. (Just the two of us – we had to take out all the seats!) This store is clever. Anyway, we bought a bunk bed and bookcases. The past few days Lawrence has been very busy putting it all together. Slowly but surely we are turning this house into our home.

A Matter Of Measure

One of the minor challenges involved in moving to a new place is the various conversions you have to deal with; Converting electricity, converting money, and converting to the metric system. This can be compounded if you are dealing with multiple conversions at once. Such as trying to get a perspective on gas prices when you are accustomed to sales in gallons to the dollar, and trying to make sense out of liters to the shekel. My favorite line was when one of my kids went to weigh herself on our old scale from America. She asked me: "Does this scale still do pounds?"

As we are quickly approaching Yom Kippur, the Day of Judgement, I hope that you all forgive me for anything I may have done to you. May the New Year bring joy, peace, health and happiness to all.

Journal Entry #39: Tuesday, September 17

Minor Purchase

I seem to have forgotten to mention a little purchase we made. We bought a car. In fact, it has been such a major focus in our lives the past month or so that it boggles my mind that I don't think I have mentioned it even once. Well, maybe I did mention it once. I mentioned it way back when we went to the Volkswagen dealer together. "Together" is the operative word here. You see, this is Laura's journal. When Lawrence goes car shopping, it doesn't always find a prominent spot in Laura's journal. After that first outing, I was bored with the whole thing, and since then Lawrence has gone to look at *every single brand of car in this country that sells a 7+*

passenger van. No joke! In fact, if you happen to need a minivan in Israel, don't even bother shopping for one. Just give us a call, and DON'T ask to speak to me, and you can get a whole spreadsheet of all of the pros and cons of everything available. I wonder if there's a market for a "Personal Minivan Shopper." Who knows? This could be our ticket! (Of course I'll just be going along for the ride...)

Oh yeah, about the car. So we bought a Hyundai H-1 (that's Yun-Die in this country). It's an Israeli-style minivan. That means it seats nine passengers. What does this mean to you? It means that when you come to Israel we can come with our whole family to pick you up at the airport and even have room for your luggage. What, you don't believe me? There's only one way to find out!

Visitors From The "Old Country"

Speaking of trips to the airport, we had our first family outing in our new car to the airport. First of all, there is something very nice about a family of six traveling in one car and no two people have to sit next to each other!

We went to the airport to greet Lawrence's mother and grandmother who are on their very first trip to Israel! How exciting for us all. What made it even more special is that they arrived with a whole group of our friends from Boca Raton who they will be touring and experiencing Israel with. How wonderful it was for us to see everyone!! We plan on joining them for at least some of the events, since we will be off the whole week of Sukkot. Great timing that we got our car right before vacation started!

The Last Place I Ever Thought I'd Find Myself...

...in the In-Flight travel magazine on EL AL. When we saw everyone at the airport they kept commenting on my picture and we didn't know what they were talking about until someone explained. They saw my picture while they were on the plane. Did you manage to catch the picture of me in the news with the smile so wide open that it looks

Featured in El Al's In-Flight travel magazine

like I'm catching flies? Well, that's in the full-page Nefesh B'Nefesh advertisement that's in El Al's magazine. So if the temptation to get a free ride home from the airport isn't enough to entice you to come to Israel, now you can see a familiar face in the in-flight magazine. Did you buy your tickets yet??

Journal Entry #40: Saturday, September 21

One Day Is Definitely Better Than Two

Today was the first day of the holiday of Sukkot. As I've mentioned, this is the holiday when we all build little huts outside and eat and sleep in them for seven days. Kind of like religious camping, I guess. Anyway, it's a lot of fun. We decorate the sukkot with lots of tinsel and strings of lights (starting to sound familiar now, isn't it?) and there are lots of feasts and parties. All of my life I celebrated Sukkot the way everyone outside of Israel does. Two days of holiday with most of the requirements of Shabbos (no working, no electricity, etc.), five intermediate days where you dress a little nicer than usual, don't go to school, go on fun trips, and, of course, eat in the sukkah, then two more days of holiday. In Israel, due to a tradition that predates modern calendars, there is only one day of "holiday," then SIX intermediate days, followed by one last day of holiday. This year, both days of holiday status come out on a Saturday. In other words, we have Shabbos, then Sunday through Friday of fun and trips and no school, then Shabbos again. I don't know if I'm explaining myself, but suffice it to say that it is a lot of fun!

An interesting twist is that if you live outside of Israel and you are in Israel for the holidays, you still have to observe those extra days. Right now my Mother-in-law and her mom are here on a trip with our synagogue from Boca Raton – and they are all keeping the second days. Tomorrow we will be joining them on a walking tour of the Old City. Of course we will *drive* to meet them, and we will have cameras and stuff, and they will not. If we're really nice maybe we will offer to take pictures with some of their cameras for them.

So why is one day better than two? Well, there is much less preparation involved so it is somewhat easier. There is also more time for trips and special events, since the kids all have off anyway. There was a part of me that felt a bit bad at missing out on another day of feasting (I always love feasting!) But there was another part of me that had a lot of fun calling every member of my family and leaving messages on their machines wishing them a good holiday, knowing they won't be getting on the phone for 30 more hours.

It's A Small World

At the dinner table of our hosts for the weekend (in Chashmonaim, a nice neighborhood about 20 miles north of Jerusalem), I told this interesting story about a man in my Ulpan class, and his experience in the Holocaust. I don't even know why I brought it up, or anything. Next morning at synagogue I looked across the way and there was that very man! I think he might actually live there!

Another one: We met a man outside the synagogue who asked us about our aliyah. We told him we came on the Nefesh B'Nefesh flight and he said he was at the reception at the airport. "In fact," he said, "maybe you remember the photo I took there? It was on the cover of the Jewish Press."

"What a coincidence," I told him, "we are the family you took the picture of!!"

Cousins, Cousins Everywhere

We moved to Israel as the first members of either of our families, so naturally we had no cousins here. But that's no fun. So we've begun to discover all sorts of cousins here. The family we stayed at for Sukkot are our cousins. How? Well, Lawrence was practically a son in the mother's parents' home growing up. That makes her practically a sister. That makes her children practically cousins!

Another family in her neighborhood are practically blood relatives! The father's sister is married to my brother. Wait, listen to this: My brother's children are *blood relatives* of both my kids, and their kids. They are cousins with the same people! That certainly makes us cousins.

Then I was put in touch with an old friend of mine who we once found out is truly my fourth-cousin-once-removed. This makes us cousins with HER whole family, and when I talked to her, she mentioned that her first cousin just made aliyah. Sooo, her *first cousin* is my *fourth-cousin-once-removed too*! Boy, do we have a lot of relatives here!!

Journal Entry #41: Monday, September 23

Tunnel Vision

Some of you may have heard about the famous(?) Tunnel Road that takes us to where we live. It is basically a bypass road so that people can get from Jerusalem to Gush Etzion and beyond without having to travel through Bethlehem. It was built with one long bridge and two tunnels that were built right into the mountains to go underneath Arab neighborhoods. Additionally there are cement barricades along various stretches of road, for instance on the bridge, to protect against any possible snipers. There is a high level of security on the road, and things have been relatively quiet for some time now. Unfortunately the Tunnel Road was built on the reputation that created its necessity and when people hear "Tunnel Road" it kind of freaks them out. Some people, that is. Other people, like my son, enter the tunnels and say, "I love the tunnel roads!" I guess it's all a matter of your perspective!

Tourists Again!! Also Titled: A Late Start Is Not A Great Start

Today we joined the Boca Raton group for a day of touring. Their scheduled time to depart the hotel was moved from 11:00 a.m. back to 10:00 a.m. So we left our house in Neve Daniel at the bright and early hour of 9:55 a.m. Whoops! It's OK, we kept telling ourselves, they NEVER leave on time. At 10:00 on the dot my mother-in-law called to find out where we are. "Don't worry," we reassured her, "we've already left the house."

Eitan enjoying Israel like a tourist

"That's good," she told us without actually knowing just how far we really were, "because they are loading the bus."

Lawrence responded by testing the accelerator in our new Hyundai. Works pretty well, I must say! Several more phone calls from a getting-impatient bus-full of Boca people and we finally arrived. I sheepishly loaded my kids onto the bus and we STILL had to wait while Lawrence found parking. I do believe they were ready to throw eggs. It was very embarrassing!

We went to Masada and Ein Gedi. Well, actually to the Dead Sea too, but I opted out of that part. 30% salt in water is much too painful on any little scratch I may have. And though I wasn't aware of having any scratches, I'm sure the water would have made me aware of any! The real reason I didn't go is because my boys would have had an even smaller appreciation of the salt in their scratches, and they're boys, so they certainly have scratches! Anyway, Masada was great. We were not given the option of climbing the snake path, only the cable car. Maybe we should be grateful! Masada was just as moving an experience today as it was 15 or so years ago when I last went. The kids enjoyed it, and my mother-in-law and her mother enjoyed it as well. (I just reminded myself: they take attendance on the bus and when they get to our family they say: "Are all four generations of Ben-Davids here?")

We stopped for lunch at the Dead Sea, then I went to collect my boys to take them on the bus to Ein Gedi. Eitan had been reluctant to come with me and I was planning on insisting, but the bus was ready to pull out and Eitan was nowhere to be found. There was NO WAY I was going to make the bus wait for me again. So I quickly told Lawrence that I was leaving Eitan and to please find him because I had no idea where he was. I got comfortable with Ezra on the bus and watched through the window as Shira ran all over searching for Eitan. I felt kind of bad leaving like that, but what could I do? We drove over to Ein Gedi and as I gathered my things the people on the bus started to offload. That's funny, I thought, that boy getting off reminds me of Eitan. Well, what do you know? It was Eitan! It took me a moment or two before I realized that poor Lawrence and Shira were still scrambling all over looking for him! One phone call later and all was well. Ein Gedi was great, and I sure am glad he came with me!

First-Time-Tourist Appreciation

After our long day, we had big appetites. We took my mother-in-law and her mother to Ben Yehudah Street. (Remember? That pedestrian mall?) How exciting it is to go someplace that is common for us, and be with someone who is seeing it for the first time. They so enjoyed it. Of course, I always enjoy it. Two and a half months and I am still in awe of where I live!! But still, this was different. We took them to an old stand-by: Café Rimon. It has a huge sukkah built around the outdoor tables and the food was plentiful and scrumptious. (Maybe I can get a job with the Jerusalem tourism industry??)

Tomorrow we leave for Tzefat (Safed) where we will be for three days. I love Sukkot vacation!!!

Journal Entry #42: Friday, September 27

Public Housing (or: The Housing That The Public Sees)

We just came back from a lovely trip up to Tzefat. Among the many things we saw were various beautiful villages, both Jewish and Arab. Something about this struck me as odd until I realized that I had been indoctrinated like the rest of the world to think that Arabs in Israel all live in sub-human slums. There no doubt is poverty here, made worse because of the Intifada. The reality is that everyone has suffered. Unemployment is the highest it's ever been for Israelis and this, I believe, is a compounded problem that has resulted from the Intifada, which caused a drastic drop in the tourism industry which has snowballed its effect in all areas. To get back to my point, Arabs live all over Israel, on both sides of the "green line", in modern, attractive towns and cities. Do they all live this way? Certainly not. Unfortunately, there are poor people from every walk of life in Israel, like any place else in the world.

On tour

Soldiers Of A Different Stripe...

While in Tzefat we noticed a sizeable gathering of Israeli soldiers who seemed rather jovial and we were curious as to what they were doing. My curiosity would take me all the way to thinking about what they might say to me if I asked them. My mother-in-law, however, went right up to them to find out. You know what? They were not a group of Israeli soldiers. They were young people from all over the world who were spending two months in Israel doing intensive basic training. Just because. They wanted to know what it was like to be in the Israeli army. Some of them were deciding to make Aliyah afterwards. All of them were connecting to their Jewish roots and to the Jewish land. None of them seemed as intense as a usual group of Israeli soldiers who are rarely found in such large numbers (around 30 or so?) in such a relaxed state.

But They Still Have A Sense Of Humor!

We were almost home today, when we drove past an army truck that was open in the back to reveal a number of Israeli soldiers being transported within. One of them was sound asleep with his head tilted back and his mouth gaping open. The guy next to him was deeply engaged in the process of carefully placing something into the sleeping soldier's mouth, while cracking up. I guess there is a time and a place for everything!!

The Christians Are Coming! The Christians Are Coming!

I truly hope I did not offend anyone by that title, but that is exactly what happened today. Since they have the long group name of "International Christian Embassy, Jerusalem" people kept calling them "The Christians," and since they were coming to visit, people were saying things like, "The Christians are coming at 3:00," or "Will you be hosting the Christians?" It was almost comical. Anyway, we hosted the Christians! Okay, I'll stop goofing around and tell you about it. It is an international group of Christians, from all denominations, who staunchly believe in the "Old Testament" (our Torah) and basically believe that Israel belongs to the Jews. They therefore do many things to support Jewish Israel, one of which is bring huge missions here, which number in the thousands. This year they had a smaller group of only 2,500 people. This amazed us since we had just come from a group of 60 and they could barely keep that group organized. "That's because they're Jews," one of the Christian visitors very correctly pointed out. So now I finally understand the difference between Jews and Christians. You thought it was Jesus? No, it's the ability of a large group of people to listen to one leader!

Anyway, back to my story. So this huge group is in Israel, and one of the things they wanted to do was to visit communities, particularly in Judea and Samaria ("over the Green Line"). So they just happened to include our community, and the community leaders picked us as one of the families to host them. Of course we were in Tzefat since Tuesday, and they were arriving today at 3:00. So we rushed home with what we thought was plenty of time, and arrived in Neve Daniel at 2:53 p.m. Forget taking showers! I ran to the little makolet (food market) in town, sent the stuff home with Lawrence, all just in time to meet our guests at the top of the hill and walk them down. Talk about a frenzy! Then we relaxed in our Sukkah, over my hastily purchased refreshments, and actually had a lovely visit. Their group provides a large amount of support, both financial and spiritual, for Israel. We were very appreciative and enjoyed their company. It was actually very interesting for us and truly a special visit that we were glad to be a part of.

Journal Entry #43: Saturday, September 28

Dancing In The Streets

Nothing like Simchat Torah in Israel! This joyful holiday which celebrates the completion of the year-long cycle of reading through the Torah in weekly portions, is fun for everyone. Outside of Israel it is celebrated on the 9th evening and the following day of the holiday of Sukkot. This would be, actually, right now. In Israel, however, as I've mentioned before, the holidays are all a day shorter due to traditions that stem from ancient calendar issues that were not a problem in Israel. So we had our Simchat Torah celebrations last night and today. Like in synagogues all over the world, the pews were moved out of the way, the mechitzas (barrier between men's and women's sections) were pushed aside, and the people sang and danced with the Torahs. The excitement was enhanced so much for me being in Israel and sharing it with my mother-in-law and her mother on their very first trip to Israel. That was yesterday.

Tonight was a whole different event. Tonight, though our holiday in Israel is technically over, this is when things really get going. Tonight, all over Israel, people had a *second* Simchat Torah celebration. Neve Daniel was no exception! On the basketball court at the top of the hill were lights, decorations, refreshments, a professional band, and enormous speakers. Hundreds from Neve Daniel and all over Gush Etzion came out for the "Second Hakafot". The men were carrying many Torah scrolls, both Ashkenazi and Sephardi ones. The music was energizing. The dancing was non-stop. People of all ages were taking part in the festivities. There were small children on their fathers' shoulders, old men dancing with their sons. There were large groups of teens, both boys and girls, who lent their own energies to the fervor. I noticed quite a few Peruvians among the celebrants. They were a group native to Peru who have the tradition of being of Jewish descent and all made aliyah this past May. Here they were with yarmulkes and their *tzitzit* (fringes) flying as they danced around. The whole thing was just amazing. I danced with the women a number of times, once, even, with my little Ezra on my shoulders. But mostly I just sat and watched and drank it all in. I hope many of you will merit to one day enjoy this special celebration too.

Journal Entry #44: Tuesday, October 1

Good One For Reader's Digest?

My son Ezra, who's now six, had a friend over to watch a video. My son suggested "Fantasia 2000."

His Israeli-born friend said, "Yeah, let's watch Fantasia!"

"Not 'Fantasia'", my son corrected, "Fantasia 2000!"

"Wow," his friend replied, "that's a lot!"

A Real Surprise Party

Speaking of Ezra, yesterday was his long-anticipated (Hebrew) birthday.

We had talked over the weekend about planning a party, and even made up a tentative guest list. On his birthday Ezra came home from school with two friends. This is not unusual and I was unperturbed. That is, until he said, "They're here for the birthday party. Should we go get the rest of the friends?"

Well, actually, err, umm...How do I get out of this without totally crushing him, I wondered? "Ezra," I proclaimed, "We have to PLAN the party! We don't even have any cake yet."

"So go make the cake!" he announced, clearly stating the obvious – to him, that is.

I took Ezra aside and explained as gently as I could that although it is his Hebrew birthday, we can still make the party on a different day. Perhaps on his English birthday. That's a great idea, I thought, as it buys me another whole week. To soothe his disappointment I suggested that he make a cake with his friends, as an activity. Maybe Shira, my 12 year-old, will help. This went over very well, and I decided to take a nap thinking that everything was all worked out and understood.

Party time!

About an hour later Shira came rushing down. Hurry Mom, you better get up!! I jumped up trying to imagine the catastrophe. Chocolate batter everywhere? A child with a cut lip? No, it was worse. Apparently Ezra hadn't understood at all. He and his two friends had gone around the neighborhood and collected the rest of his friends. After all, in his mind the only problem had been the lack of cake. Now that was solved, and the party could go on! I had a moment where I imagined how I was going to send all of those children home, when I realized, Hey! I've got pizza in the freezer, birthday candles in the drawer, even a little art activity that will provide each child with something (very cheap!) to take home. Let's have a party! So party we did. It may be the first surprise party on record where the surprise was on the person *throwing* the party!

Hey...Watch Where You're Going!!

Actually, maybe *I* should. The other day at Ulpan I was walking with

Lawrence during our break and we must have been having a very deep and involved conversation. I don't know what it was about, but apparently I was very interested in what I had to say for I didn't notice where I was until Lawrence looked at me and said, "This is the Men's Room." Whoops!

Another Whoops At Ulpan...

...but this time it was somebody else's. I don't know who, but it's someone who must have learned to drive yesterday, for he made a nice, big scratch all around the rear corner fender and above on our new bus, I mean, car. At first we behaved like angry Americans: Who did this?! Look what he did!! I can't believe he just left the scene!! Then we remembered where we are and realized that our car is just not going to be a fashion statement (not that it ever was!) and that even if we wanted to, we can't even sell it for five years, so just GET USED TO IT! There, that felt better. I do have a nice, new bumper sticker. Maybe if I just position it at a slight angle I can cover up the dent just a bit......

Journal Entry #45: Tuesday, October 8

Old Places Have Lots Of New Appeal

When my mother-in-law and her mom were here, we naturally went to the mall (isn't that what all women do??). Then we decided that there are other shopping experiences that have a little more of an Israeli flavor: First stop, Machane Yehudah!! For the uninitiated, this is a classic Middle Eastern outdoor *shuk*. Every fresh smell imaginable all mingle together in this colorful, noisy, bustling market; from fresh bread to fresh fish. Of course, we went on a day of a heat wave so you can add fresh sweat to the mix. There was every kind of nut and spice; fruits and vegetables; even music, electronics and clothing. Having been the target of suicide bombers in the past, many people now avoid this historic market. It is now enclosed with security at every entrance, and does not seem to have suffered any loss to its character. I will strongly recommend that you use the bathroom *before* you go to this remnant from another era.

Another shopping trip through time was in Mea Shearim. This old, Jerusalem neighborhood of Hasidic/Hareidi/Ultra-Orthodox Jews is famous for its super-narrow cobblestone streets, little shops selling every type of Judaica dotting every alley, and signs informing all visitors to dress modestly. As we strolled and shopped, my mother-in-law looked around and decided she would love to get an apartment in Mea Shearim. She might have to make a few minor lifestyle changes, but it's a great location!!

Israel Is Great; The Hotdogs Could Use Some Work

One great thing about living in Israel is the wide variety of kosher food available. For example, at the Jerusalem mall, I can go to the food court and not only get ice cream, but my choice of just about anything from pizza to burgers to falafel and even Thai food. All under the strictest standards of *kashrut* (kosher)! In fact, when we go there as a family, we split up and everyone gets the food they want and we meet back at the tables.

I decided to try a "famous" Nathan's hotdog. Great idea! All-American, real beef, tasty hotdog. So I ordered a couple of #2's from Nathan's. "Where's the mustard?" I asked the vendor. "Oh, you want mustard?" he asked in a surprised tone. Then he dug out a few packets from a box that looked like it had been buried a long time. I guess mustard is not as popular as tehina around here. He handed me a tray with long cylinder packets – they twisted waxed paper around each end of the dog, so you could see the length based on the bun, but it was totally wrapped. Wow. I thought, these are some nice long hotdogs! To my surprise, the buns were almost double the length of the hotdogs.

Can you imagine? Nathan's sells hotdogs that don't match its own buns.

This One Will Really Get Your Goat!

A neighbor of ours (who we don't yet know) just got a pet that has a remarkable resemblance to our own unusual looking dog, Teeka. (Who we still have, but are looking for another home for, but that's another story). Anyway this pet is about the same size, same rich, chocolate brown color, short-haired, and – would you believe it? – even has a similar beard! The major difference between our pet and theirs? Their pet is a goat. A goat. Why? I don't know why. But the first time Lexi saw the goat, it was being walked by one of the girls in the family.

Lexi said to the girl: "Why are you walking a goat?"

Girl: "Because it needs to get out every once in a while."

Journal Entry #46: Wednesday, October 9

Public Speaking Double Whammy

My Ulpan class has a daily feature called the "Friend of the Day". I'm sure you all know what that is. You did it in first grade, right?? Anyway, today I was the "friend of the day". I prepared my little speech and decided to use the topic of how I came to make Aliyah. (I wondered what the Arab guy in my class was thinking while I gave my shpiel). Of course I was nervous all morning in anticipation of speaking in public. Even though it was only twenty-five people. To me, if it's more than an audience of three, it's public speaking!! Oh, and I imagine you realize that this speech of mine had to be entirely in Hebrew. Well, the time came, I got up my nerve, and did my thing (entirely from a prewritten speech! It takes me five minutes to compose each sentence, so I had to do it in advance.) They all clapped at the end so I guess it was OK, but then again, whose didn't they clap for? Fine, so I finished. I showed them some pictures of me, my family, siblings, parents, etc. Then it was time to go.

Next stop was back to Neve Daniel, but we were to be meeting with a group of sixty people from South Africa on a pilot trip to Israel. "Do we need to prepare anything?" I had asked my husband a week ago when I heard we were doing this. "No," he insisted, "we will simply be meeting with them." This was good, because I was not at all excited about speaking publicly twice in one day. We arrived as the two busloads were piling into the Neve Daniel social hall. I went over to check in with the coordinator and double checked that he did not expect us to speak. "Yes, I do expect you to speak," he replied to me, my eyes wide with shock and my mouth gaping open.

Great, I thought, this gives us exactly 30 seconds to prepare what to say. At least I didn't have that "nervous all morning" thing. But wait, I was nervous all morning anyway. You think it could have been worse?? Well, we did it. I spoke, and we both answered a lot of questions. At least this time it was in English! I have actually maintained for the past six months or so, that I want to speak out for Aliyah, and how can one accomplish this without speaking?? (Very easily, actually – write an internet journal!!) Anyway, I think today was a success, and maybe it was better that we didn't plan – we spoke from the heart.

This Says It All

When I finished speaking, a South African gentleman asked me an interesting question regarding our Aliyah. He asked: "I know why we leave, but why did you leave?" (He was referring to the high crime and various difficulties facing Jews in South Africa).

I answered him, "We didn't *leave* anything. Coming to Israel was simply an *arrival*."

Journal Entry #47: Saturday, October 12

Whatever Happened To "Apple Pie And Chevrolet"?

After fourteen years of marriage, the I.R.S. finally decided that I cannot file a tax return without putting my married name on my social security card. (The married name that I no longer use since I moved to Israel!) So we prepared for a trip into East Jerusalem (the Arab side of the tracks) to go to the American Consulate. Aside from being in a neighborhood that you DON'T want to get a flat tire in, we figured it must be a very safe place once inside. You know, Marines, American officials in suits, a little American oasis in the Middle East. This is what we *figured.* Were we ever wrong!!

The first thing that struck us was that all of the American citizens arriving when we did were Arabs. The next thing that struck us is that there were no Marines, no American officials in suits, in fact, there were no Americans at all! Everyone working there was Arab!! What's going on? We wondered. Isn't this the American consulate? There was no one there who even spoke English with an American accent!

Then while Abdullah was helping me with my social security card paperwork, I noticed a few "free copies" of a periodical magazine on his desk. I asked him for a copy, which he gave me with a bit of an odd glance. Perhaps, because I was quite obviously a religious Jew and the magazine was "This Week in Palestine." This is a magazine that you can pick up for free at OUR American Consulate. And what a magazine it was! My favorite article was the one by the Christian Palestinian woman who wrote about her deep sympathies for the victims of the suicide bombings and how it is "all Sharon's fault."

Oh wait; I almost forgot the best part: The American consulate in East Jerusalem, by policy, will ONLY hire Arabs. An American institution. And an official one, no less. Could you imagine an American government office that only hired Blacks? Or only women? How about if they only hired Catholics? Or Harry Potter fans? It's so un-American that we were flabbergasted.

Journal Entry #48: Tuesday, October 15

On The Radio

What can I say? I found my favorite radio station. It plays a great mix of English music, not just the new stuff. The news is all in English. I get excellent reception – even when I'm driving. It sounds perfect. It just happens to be Radio Jordan. As in: the country. Look, I listen to the news with a big boulder of salt. It's actually somewhat interesting to hear both Israeli and American news, told from the Arabs' perspective. Believe me, I've been trying to find a good Israeli radio station. The other day, I set off from Neve Daniel, alone, to pick up Lawrence in Jerusalem. I fiddled with the stations and found a song that I loved, playing on some radio station. I turned up the volume and was all happy to be able to take a nice drive with great music. All of a sudden, bzzzzzzzz. No reception. I waited a few minutes, ever hopeful that when I turned the next corner it would come back. It never did. Oh well. Now I listen to Old Faithful: Radio Jordan.

It's A Small World After All

I went to *shul* (synagogue) on Shabbos and a neighbor came over to me and said you must come and meet my guest. Why? Apparently his wife told him about me after she read my journals, which she got from a friend, who got them from my father. (I think.) She knew he was going to Neve Daniel, where I live and it's a VERY small town.

Torah Dedication And Lots Of Cousins

Yesterday we had the honor of attending a beautiful ceremony for the dedication of a new Torah scroll to the Israel Defense Forces (I.D.F.). It was a very special event attended by none other than Rabbi Lau, Chief Rabbi of Israel. The reason we went is because the family who donated the Torah are our cousins. Distant cousins. Okay, the ones who are my age are my fourth-cousins-once-removed. Then we got to meet more cousins since most of the people related to them, are related to me as well. Besides for expanding my family tree, it was a very meaningful event that we were pleased to be a part of.

A Bad Habit Getting Worse

Lawrence and I continue to go to Ulpan (our Hebrew language classes) every day. Classes start at the much too early hour of 8 a.m. Not that I should complain, since I have NEVER been there that early. The earliest has been 8:10. Usually it's been more like 8:30. But lately we've just been shlepping along and barely make it there by 9 a.m. Now we've gotten really bad. As we get closer to the building each morning, we start trying to think if there is anything at all that we need to do instead of going to Ulpan. It's not that it's so boring or terrible or anything, but, well, you know. It IS school.

My class, in particular, is getting quite tedious as our main text that we work with is the newspaper. I mean, we pick the thing apart. Not that I'm not glad to be getting the skills necessary to read the newspaper, but a bit of cheerful reading would be nice as well!

Three Month Review

(Can you believe it's been so long?) My kids are adjusting beautifully to school. They are all receiving extra help with their Hebrew. Each one is integrating with the neighborhood children, the girls are involved in the youth group (B'nei Akiva), and they all seem to be happy. As for us? We are thrilled!! We are so happy to be in Israel, we live in a beautiful area, we have made great friends, and what more do we need? Well, actually, jobs would be nice. We have started to look seriously into job prospects and we will see what happens with that.

Journal Entry #49: Wednesday, October 16

A Miracle!!!

What I'm about to tell you can certainly be titled "What a Bummer!" or "Our Bad News For The Day", but when you hear the story you will understand why even the police officer called it nothing short of a miracle.

Around 1:50 this afternoon, a time when few cars are on the road, but many small children are walking home from nursery school, Lawrence and I were in our kitchen, minding our own business, when I noticed what seemed like a truck moving very quickly down the hill past my house. Next thing I heard was a distinct crash and I instinctively ran to my window to reassure myself that my own car was safe and sound in our parking spot. Except that it wasn't. In fact, it wasn't even in the parking spot. My car had vanished altogether. I motioned to Lawrence who was on the phone to come outside and we dashed out thinking that the crash was coincidental, and that our car was stolen. We were wrong. Our car wasn't stolen at all. But it was about 20 meters away from where we'd parked it, up on the sidewalk, and completely smashed in the rear. The culprit? A runaway truck that didn't listen to its driver, but carefully followed the rules of gravity and inertia and hurtled down into our car, smashing it and pushing it to where it ended up, then veering to the left and continuing on further down the hill until it somehow ended up past the community fence and flipped upside down.

So what's the miracle? Well, judging from the path of the truck, had our car not been where it was, the truck would probably not have veered to the left and would have been in a direct collision course with a house. But that's only the first one. Remember the "many small children walking home from nursery school"? Not one child was touched. No one was hurt. Not even a scratch. Well, that's not completely true. The driver of the truck, who managed to jump out of the truck in time, got a few scratches when he climbed back *into* the truck to get his registration.

Oh, and about those scratches. You see, the driver was of a group of Arab workers working on our friends' house next door. As a rule, we kind of mind our own business and stay away from each other. This may not follow the rules of etiquette in the Western world, in fact it doesn't really sit well with me either, but there is a kind of a war here, so we try to just keep things quiet. Anyway, so this driver dude was standing in front of my house with these scratches and I brought out some hydrogen peroxide and cotton for him to clean it up with. As I'm handing them to him, he turns his scratched arm to me expecting me to clean it for him, maybe thinking I'm Florence Nightingale or something. Well I am a nurse *you* know. There was a momentary awkward pause as I thought that Arab or no Arab, he's a big boy and he can clean up his own wound, but, I did it anyway.

Journal Entry #50: Saturday, October 19

Out Of The Woodwork

Not that people here aren't always nice and helpful, because they are. But since our little car mishap (which was "headline" news in this little town!) people have been going out of their way to offer us rides to the store or anything else we might need. The best offer was from someone who just bought a new car and hasn't sold the old one yet, so, at least for a few days, we have a car to use. People have also been offering their condolences, and I find I have to comfort *them* and say it's only a car!

Oh, and about the car. We had included towing in our insurance policy, so we promptly called to take advantage of it. Except that we weren't in their system, and they said they weren't coming. We got a taste of what's ahead when we went back and forth calling the insurance company and the towing company, speaking to people of varying degrees of knowledge of English. Finally, it all straightened out, and the tow truck came. Now the challenge will be to get them to total the car. If they fix the car, we will have a car that will probably always have problems, and will be extremely devalued if we ever want to sell it. However, if we total the car, we will need to sue the guy's insurance company for (get ready for this, it's higher mathematics) what *we* paid for the car, PLUS the amount of the *tax break* we received as new immigrants (since we would technically be buying our *second* car, and could not get it with the special new immigrant tax break) PLUS the amount of the tax break a *second time* since we would be "selling" our first car in less than the required five-year term and would be obligated to pay the full amount of the original tax break! (Did *you* get all that? It had to be explained to me three times).

Of course all of this suing and whatever else could be done in an efficient and organized way can be done by one's insurance broker. That is, of course, if one had the foresight and fortune of having one in the first place. We did not. When we got our car we shopped for the best price in insurance and got it through a company similar to what we had in the states. You know, every time you call you speak to someone different. Except that it doesn't work in this situation. Imagine that you are suing someone and instead of hiring a lawyer, you just hire a big company and every time you call you speak to a different lawyer!! We are doing exactly that. AND we don't speak the language! This is going to be fun....

Journal Entry #51: Sunday, October 20

The Other Side Of The Fence

On Friday morning, as I was arriving home, I saw a most unusual sight. You see, we live in a gated community. Not gated as in Boca Raton, Florida. Not gated as in golf course, country club and Porsche. This is a different kind of gated. This is keep-out-the-Arabs gated. Of course, as you all know, there are plenty of Arabs INSIDE our community. Like the ones who were working next door with the runaway truck. Anyway, back to Friday morning. As I was arriving home, I noticed several Arabs at the fence right near our house. Both on the inside and on the outside! My first reaction was: Intruders!!! Then I remembered that a huge chunk of the gate had been flattened by a certain truck that thought it could fly. So these Arabs were working. They were here to fix the gate. Our protective gate. In other words, the Arabs were fixing the gate so that the Arabs can't get in. Hmmm. Let me think about that one...

Hebrew Challenges

Each week Ezra, my Kindergartener, comes home with a newsletter about what they learned and what they need to bring for the next week. This is about the most difficult part of my week. The entire thing is in Hebrew, and they're learning about things like the Equator and the "Iron Curtain". (In Kindergarten!! Can you imagine?) So I struggle through some of it, and pay special attention to the "what they need to bring for next week" section. It seemed to me that they were supposed to be bringing in photos of their families or something like that. So I dutifully put together a little packet of a variety of pictures to make sure that something I sent was the right thing. This was early last week. Then on Friday I met with Ezra's teacher and while in the classroom I noticed something very interesting. There, on the bulletin board, was a lovely picture gallery with all of Ezra's pictures. And no one else's!! Did I totally misunderstand the note? What was she thinking when I sent in all those pictures?

Is it possible that the one parent in 25 who doesn't speak Hebrew was the only one who followed the directions? That would be nice.

Oh well. It is a very nice photo gallery!

Journal Entry #52: Monday, October 21

How Bad Is A Demotion?

I think I've had it with my Ulpan. The level I'm in is entirely devoted to learning the words used in the news. This means that I spend four hours a day, every day, hashing over the news. Does this sound like fun? I just want to be able to talk to my kids' teachers, doctors, decline telemarketers, and order great desserts in the cafes. What more do I need? Of course I have to get over the ego thing...

Teeka May Soon Be Taken??

FINALLY the guy who found Teeka for us is trying to find someone else for Teeka. We spoke to a woman tonight who wants to see her but she won't drive to where we live. A minor detail. One that WILL be worked out, I assure you!!

Neve Daniel's Claim To Fame

Not the magnificent view; not the proximity to Jerusalem; not the cozy feeling of a small village nestled on a mountain top; not the beautiful red-tile roofed homes sided with Jerusalem stone. No, I'm talking about the fog. Hey, I never said anything about the "top selling point," merely its "claim to fame." Or one of them, anyway. (Wind rates pretty high up there as well!)

So this morning I ventured out in Neve Daniel-style pea soup fog. Why is this fog different from all other fogs, you ask? Because it is mixed with that aforementioned wind. So not only you can't see ten feet in front of you, but the wind does a great job of making sure you don't know which way "in front of you" is. I pulled the car away tentatively (very tentatively – it was not my car!) and started making my way through it all. I only went off the road two or three times. Anyway, the amazing thing is that as you start driving down the mountain away from Neve Daniel, you drive right out of the fog. Today it was like that, in any case. As I understand, this will be our weather for quite a while. Luckily I always liked pea soup...

Journal Entry #53: Wednesday, October 23

Conspicuous Absence

You know what I haven't seen much of lately? Ghouls, goblins, witches and Jack-o-lanterns. In fact, I haven't seen any. I almost forgot we were in October! It's a really neat thing to be in a country where the holidays I celebrate, and pretty much ONLY those holidays, are what *you* see and hear about. Not that I have anything against cultural diversity, but no matter how hard the U.S. tries to inject Chanukah and Kwanzaa into December, Christmas still rules! (As it should, being that America is a predominantly Christian country, lest we forget…) Anyway, I wouldn't mind all those extra bags of candy that we all seem to stock up on right about now (especially all those post-Halloween sales) but I can't say I'm exactly being deprived (as I munch on an Egozi bar…)

Demotion Accomplished…(And Boy, Am I Glad!)

We arrived at Ulpan as usual this morning (read: late) and I went straight to the principal's office. I nervously explained to her that I would like to switch classes. "But Ariella," she said in Hebrew that I tried to understand, "which class would *you* switch to?" As if I would possibly move UP a class. She tried to talk me out of it, but I was quite sure at that point. So she gave me my little permission slip, and I tentatively walked into the "Gimel" (level 3) class. Whoa! It was completely different. I sat through a lengthy explanation of grammar concepts that were quite easy for me, and I wondered what I had done. But then, people started speaking. An amazing thing in that class made all the difference: Hardly anyone speaks English!! You don't understand – it doesn't matter WHAT they're learning in that class. As long as everything is in Hebrew! Even when we break into small groups, in this class I will have NO CHOICE but to speak in Hebrew. In the higher level class? With mostly Americans? We break into groups and that's the end of the Hebrew! The other great thing is that I don't have to spend so much time dwelling on the news!

Journal Entry #54: Thursday, October 24

Now THIS Is A Class Trip!

But before I get into all that, there is something very unique about the class trips here. They invite the fathers to go instead of the mothers. This is because mothers carry babies, and fathers carry guns. (Much more formidable weapons in case one is G-d forbid necessary.) In fact we know of a dad who was invited to go on his daughter's trip, and when he got there the teachers looked at him in surprise, and said "Where is your gun?!" And he thought they invited him for his charm and good looks...

In any event, my kids are accustomed to a rich array of exciting class trips. Everything from the local bank to Disney World. But THIS – this was something else entirely. My daughter went on a class trip to Bethlehem – to *Kever Rachel (*The Tomb of Rachel, the matriarch). I would tell you all about it but since I'm not a gun-toting-Dad I wasn't invited, so I have asked Lexi to share a few words with you herself:

"People would think that it's really scary to go to Kever Rachel because it's in an Arab place. I was scared but it didn't stop me from going. It felt so good to go to Kever Rachel because it's where one of my 'mothers' is buried. And it was very special for me to go and to think that not a lot of people have gone there [lately – because of the situation]. It is special because since the Intifada is happening people have to go with special army escorts and me and my grade went with a few men with guns and that's it. They were dads of the girls in my class. It felt so special to be there, to think that this is where my mother [matriarch] is buried and I was *davening* [praying]. It felt like I was talking to her and to Hashem. It was amazing that even though it's really old, it looks outstanding on the inside. There are chandeliers everywhere. The walls are being painted often. And there are different sections for the men and women. Most of all, it was very special to share all of what I did that day with my friends. If you come to Israel, you should try to go to Kever Rachel."

What more can I say? She said it all!

Journal Entry #55: Thursday, October 24, part 2

Only In Israel

We went out to dinner with friends last night and while searching for a restaurant came upon a Thai place that we thought we would check out. "What's the difference between the two seating sections?" our friend asked the Maitre D'.

"In this section, smoking is not allowed," he answered indicating the section we were in. Then he added: "In that section smoking is also not allowed. But people smoke."

I couldn't help but laugh. I also couldn't help but leave. After all, if there's a smoking section anywhere, there's a *smoke* section everywhere!

The Brighter Side Of Laundry

Having a family of six, managing the laundry seems to have always been one of those unreachable goals. Until I arrived in Israel. Was it possible that my excitement about making Aliyah was so strong that it made the laundry go smoother? Or perhaps it was the fact that I finally had a brand new washing machine and dryer? Well, no, it's neither of those two. Upon careful reflection I came up with the real reason laundry is so much easier. I have several huge, new laundry hampers that can each take many days before overflowing! I don't have to start doing laundry until people run out of clothes! (Seriously!! I recommend this for everyone!)

Laura Leaves Ulpan Class And Rumors Abound

This morning, at Ulpan, everyone I saw from my previous class approached me with one version or another of the "official" reason as to why I left the class. It varied from "too much English spoken" to "too many Americans" (I loved that one). The funny thing was that most of those English-speaking former classmates of mine approached me speaking Hebrew! (I guess that rumor produced quite a bit of guilt!)

Journal Entry #56: Sunday, October 27

No Shortchanging When Chanukah Is Early

America has made quite an attempt to equalize Chanukah with Christmas. Not that they are equal or have anything remotely to do with each other. Outside of Israel you will see (in high Jewish concentration areas, anyway) the token menorah, Jewish star, or Happy Chanukah sign blended in with all the wreaths and trees and holly. In some places it's even quite elaborate. That's all well and good, except when Chanukah starts at the end of November and Christmas season is only just beginning.

Ah! But in Israel Chanukah season starts a month before – well, Chanukah of course! In fact when I began to notice *sufganiyot* (jelly doughnuts – traditional Chanukah treats) in all of the stores and it was still October, I had a hard time relating it to Chanukah myself! But how cool is it that the whole country gears up together for every holiday! (MY holidays!)

Great Way To Ax The Taxes

In Israel we pay a high tax on pretty much everything and it is known by its acronym MA"M (in Hebrew letters of course) – rhymes with "Tom".

Anyway, partly for this reason many American's living in Israel choose to get a lot of merchandise in America and have it sent to them rather than buying here. I guess it can be said that when you get things in Israel, you pay MA"M. When you get things from America, Mom pays.

Another Funny Story

A French couple recently made Aliyah to Neve Daniel and was totally reliant on either rides from friends or buses for transportation. (F.Y.I. The name of the main bus company here is "Egged") Anyway, the first time they were waiting for a bus to Neve Daniel, it took a very long time, while buses to other places kept on passing them. After a number of these buses passed by, the husband commented to his wife in frustration, "Why did we have to move to Neve Daniel, which hardly has any buses? Why couldn't we have moved to Egged instead?"

Language Challenge

Someone asked Shira how she was doing in school with the language and such. She answered that it is so difficult to understand that sometimes she has to ask the girl next to her just to find out what *subject* they're in!

Privacy: A Limited Privilege Around Here

Did you know that when you go on a job interview in Israel they can, and usually do, ask you just about anything they want? Like how old you are, how much money you make, and how much you weigh. (Well, maybe not that...) It's pretty much like that everywhere you go around here. People are blunt and direct and expect everyone else to be as well. Anyway, at my ulpan class yesterday the teacher was giving back our tests (my first!) so she told the first person as she handed it to him: Great job! And to the next person: Very nice! And the next: Tsk, tsk, what happened? And then: (with a shake of the head) Very bad. I watched as she commented to every single person, out loud, how they had done. I thought that perhaps next time, she may as well post all of our tests, with her comments, on the bulletin board!

Journal Entry #57: Monday, October 28

Anglos Predominantly Speak – Why, Hebrew Of Course!

In Neve Daniel, that is. I went to a meeting last night to help organize a nice women's event here in Neve Daniel. We met at an American woman's home; present were another American, me, a South African woman, and a French woman and one Israeli. Obviously, it should be an English-speaking meeting, right? Wrong. It was 90% in Hebrew. Don't get me wrong – I was thrilled. There is nothing easier than understanding an American speaking

Hebrew. But it is VERY difficult to SPEAK to an American in Hebrew!

Wild Party At Ulpan

Today one of the Ulpan classes had an engagement party for a guy in their class. During break they invited everyone in to share in the ample food and beverages. Oh, and about those beverages: they had hard alcohol in their classroom! I didn't see the selection, but Lawrence had a shot of single-malt scotch. I bet the rest of his lessons today were a little more pleasant than usual!

Just realize that in these Ulpans there are quite a number of barely-out-of-high-school kids. Can you imagine? As I've said before, only in Israel!

License To...Drive!

Guess what I got in the mail today. My official, genuine, brand-spanking new, Israeli driver's license! No more temporary slip-of-paper license! The best part? The picture. I know, that's supposed to be the worst part that one is obligated to complain about, especially if one is a woman. But not this woman! You see, in Israel you can take your license picture with a hat on – so I get to proudly display my Yankees hat whenever I show my license!

Journal Entry #58: Tuesday, October 29

Taste Of Israeli Medicine

As in "The System", not as in "antibiotics." Of course this should happen on a day that we still have no car. One of my kids called from school with a backache. We were hitching a ride to Ulpan and I was *about* to get into the car when she called. So I ditched Ulpan and hitched a ride to her school instead. We went to the doctor (around the corner from her school) expecting the "take two and call me in the morning" routine, but instead he thought she should see an Orthopedist and have an x-ray. Oh, and did I mention that this had to be done in Jerusalem? Of course, the doctor added, you don't want to take her on buses. All that jostling won't be good for her. You do have a car, don't you?

"Well," I sheepishly admitted, "we have a car but it's been in the shop for two weeks now."

"Then you must get a ride from someone," he said with finality.

So I sat with my cell phone and called everyone I had put in its memory who lived within ten minutes of the doctor's office. Luckily, I found a car to borrow – from an extremely nice person who had to come all the way to get us and bring himself back home!! The end of the story is I found my way, it turned out that she was fine (the doctor in the Urgent Care place gave us the "take two..." routine), we picked up Lawrence from Ulpan, and we all went home.

When We Got Home

The first thing we noticed was that our electricity was out and apparently had been for some time. No problem, we thought, this happens here all the time and someone always seems to fix it without our even making a call. It will be on before long. Wrong! Apparently this was not your run-of-the-mill-blackout. This was your landlord-never-paid-the-electricity-bill-blackout! Since May! Furious, but stuck, Lawrence paid the whole balance on our credit card (appropriate parts of which will be coming off our next rent check, thank you very much!) Luckily the power people turned our electricity back on three hours before the 7 p.m. time they'd initially told us they would.

More Landlord Fun

Speaking of our rent check, the electricity bill isn't all that we'll be taking off of the amount. Our landlord was finally kind enough to get us a door for our bedroom. Well, she didn't exactly *get* the door. She just ordered it. Well, she didn't exactly order the door either, so I'm not exactly sure what she did, other than *tell us* she ordered it, because Lawrence shlepped out to pick it up, but no such order existed. So Lawrence selected the door, paid for it (coming off that next rent check!) and brought it home. BUT – the door didn't fit. Absolutely nothing about it fit. It didn't fit in the frame, the hinges didn't match up to the ones in the wall, nothing! (Incidentally, when we checked the doors in the rest of the house, none of them were standard size and none of them even matched each other!) He could have just gotten a slab of wood and made a new door (which is more or less what he did anyway). Two hours later, we have a bedroom door. (and we'll take two hours labor off the rent check too...)

Closing The Fish Bowl

As long as we were putting up a door on our bedroom, we thought that maybe it was about time that we put curtains up as well. It's only been three months since we bought the curtains. They needed a minor sewing job. Problem was, I don't sew and I don't have a sewing machine. Since we were on a roll, we found a neighbor to borrow a sewing machine from, I got a crash course in sewing a straight line, and I whipped those curtains into shape! Now, amazingly enough, we can actually be in our bedroom and no one can see inside it! I call that progress.

Journal Entry #59: Friday, November 1

Another Great School Story

The other day in Lexi's class, the teacher was dictating as the girls were writing.

"Too fast!" several girls complained.

Ever the problem solver, Lexi suggested to the teacher, "Why don't you just write the words on the board?"

The whole class burst into laughter as one of the girls explained, "Lexi, this is a spelling test!!"

It's Only Been 16 Days…

Well, we finally picked up our car today. Not bad, the estimator was only off by 22,000 shekels (about $4,500 – and that's just what he was *off* by!). We put the whole darn thing on our American Express card, hoping that the system really works and that the other guy's insurance will send us a check before the bill comes. Lawrence had checked the car last night and instructed the guy to make a few more minor repairs, so when we went to get the car we expected it to be perfect. Nope! What wasn't perfect? Where should I begin? The back door wasn't aligned right, there were still glass flecks all over, a scratch (that wasn't there in the first place!) was supposed to have been repaired, and some panel inside wasn't attached. And this was all on first glance! (Not that we expected less with 42,000 shekels in repairs!) Anyway, we pointed this all out to the foreman, who sent a guy over with a can of paint to first deal with the scratch. Lawrence then pointed out the misaligned door to the serviceman, who proceeded to use his *hands* to try to straighten out the door. In so doing, he actually made a *new dent* on the door! We watched this all, flabbergasted, and immediately complained to the foreman.

The foreman said "Why did you let him touch the door? All he does is paint!"

But he promised to fix all of the leftover problems, *and* the new dent, after the weekend. At least we have our car!!

Journal Entry #60: Sunday, November 3

Hey, Israel Has Culture!

Today I took my girls and six others from our neighborhood to see the ballet "Coppelia." So what, that the usually twenty-five minute drive to Jerusalem took us almost an hour because security was so tight that they were checking nearly every car? We still got there! (Better late than never, right?) Coppelia was as wonderful tonight, as I remember it 20 years ago with my mom and my aunt in Manhattan. The only difference this time was that we had third row seats AND it only cost about $5.20 per ticket. You can't even go to a movie for that price! While it wasn't exactly the Royal Ballet, it was a wonderful performance and it was enjoyed by all.

A New Breed Of Terrorist Has Come To Town...

...the four legged kind. Neve Daniel has been invaded by RABIES! No joke, this is really a big problem. Our very close friends woke up early on Friday to discover their very big dog being attacked by a scrappy mongoose. It sounded like a rabid animal attack to everyone, but we all hoped for a better outcome. The second dog that was attacked managed to kill the thing, and it was tested for rabies. Unfortunately, it tested positive. This is not very good news for the two dogs who were attacked (at least one was late getting her rabies shot). It is also a problem for the dogs' families who had handled their attacked dogs. Almost everyone in my friend's family has to have a whole series of rabies shots now. But there's more. First of all, there are many stray cats in the neighborhood, any of which might be carrying the disease and infecting other animals and/or people. Like the little boy around the corner who was scratched by a cat and now needs to be treated for rabies. And, like our Teeka for instance. Wait a minute; this definitely needs its own paragraph.

Teeka's Paragraph

You won't believe this. We got a call yesterday from the guy who found Teeka for us. He told us he had a family in Jerusalem who was interested in Teeka. So Lawrence put Teeka in the car and drove her off to Jerusalem. And would you believe it? They kept her!! So that's the good news. Now for the rest. You see, Teeka had a great fondness for cats. And I don't mean that they were among her closest circle of friends. In fact, Teeka has killed three cats to date. Besides that it was horrible, gross, and all that, we now have a different problem. What if one of her unfortunate victims had *rabies*? This is not only a potential problem for her, but a potential problem for us as well. And we just gave her to new owners!! First thing tomorrow we need to call the Ministry of Health and find out what we need to do. Can you imagine? All this comes to light on the *very day* that we finally have found a new home for Teeka?? More to come on this, I'm sure...

Journal Entry #61: Tuesday, November 5

NOT A Deja Vu

Sitting in Ulpan today, our class suddenly heard what sounded like a huge explosion followed by screams right outside our window. Everyone, teacher included, ran from their seats to the window expecting to see the worst. I was shaking with adrenaline, I had that feeling of "something must be done but I don't know what." We looked for smoke, listened for sirens, and tried to locate evidence of what had possibly occurred to create such a terrible explosion. The teacher ran for a radio but we heard nothing unusual. No breaking stories, no dreadful announcements of suicide attacks. On looking out the window we determined that the screams we had heard came from the ever-loitering high school kids, who (sometimes) attend school at the site of our Ulpan, as an instant reaction to the powerful noise. At this point they were all laughing and carrying on as usual, while we were all scurrying about our classroom waiting to hear the bad news. Our teacher finally reassured us that if there is no breaking news announcement, then there is no news and we should just relax. However, she did stop class several more times to listen to the radio.

How we felt for that half hour of the false alarm (I still don't know what it was) only reminded me of how I felt on September 11th of last year. Then I was the teacher, and my class of little three-year-olds was blissfully ignorant of the fact that I had my eyes and one ear on them, while the other ear was plastered to the speaker of a radio that they didn't even know was on. Unfortunately, that was the real thing and my being 1200 miles away in Florida didn't lessen the pain for me at all.

Is This Russia Or Israel?

And I wasn't referring to the fact that now many signs, food items and stores have added Russian after the Hebrew, Arabic and English, or the fact that with all the Russian immigrants here, Russian is becoming a very popular language. Actually I was referring to old Russia, as in the former U.S.S.R. What made me think of that? Well, last night I went to pick up some simple packages that my parents sent to me – and they were opened! I don't mean like by accident. I mean that there was perfectly secure tape that had been slit open and not even retaped. Just a plastic strap was holding the boxes barely closed. I suppose they were looking for items that were new and required taxes to be paid on (which there were quite a few of!) but somehow, though they bothered opening it all, they didn't do anything about it. Unless a bill is on its way to me in the mail!

The Final(?) Verdict On Teeka

So Lawrence started to feel guilty about sending off our dog when there's a possibility of rabies. He decided to go and get Teeka back, get her the rabies booster shot, and then return her. I thought he was nuts; that we should just casually mention to them that rabies is going around and they might want to get a booster. Well, Lawrence first called the guy who both found Teeka for us, and then found the new owners for her, and he said to absolutely NOT take Teeka back, just tell them and let them deal. As for all of us who have had contact with an animal that might have had contact with an animal that had rabies, and having not been the victims of any sign of aggression, we were told to forget about it and not worry about things that don't exist for us. As for our friends, though, they are all going through with a difficult rabies inoculation schedule, and their dog will be in isolation for six months!

Journal Entry #62: Saturday, November 9

What A Month!

At least I get my girls back after tonight. Today was the culmination of a month-long event called *Chodesh Irgun.* Don't worry; I didn't have a clue what it was either. It basically means "The month of organizing" (not that tonight's main event was particularly organized, but more on that later) and is participated in by branches of the youth group *B'nei Akiva* all across the country. The evening began with a beautiful ceremony. Hundreds of people gathered at the outdoor basketball court in Neve Daniel and watched from perches on the wall (Really, this was where we sat!) as dozens of young teens performed a wonderful ceremony using huge Israeli flags. It was truly a sight to see!

Shira's wonderful performance

Of course, the reason we had gone was to see our daughters performing in each of their respective age groups. The event started at 7:45 p.m. We were five minutes late. At 8:55, the event seemed to end and everyone started to leave. Horrified, I asked my friend if I could have possibly missed my daughters' performance, if it might have been at the beginning. Not to worry, she said. The show hasn't even started. We're only moving to another location. And so we did. In fact, by the time it did start my boys were falling asleep, and my girls were 5th and 7th in the lineup! Unfortunately by the fourth act, one was asleep and the other going nuts, so Lawrence escaped with both of them and I stayed. Until 11:00! And it was still going strong!! But as soon as my kids were done, I was outta' there! Believe me, it was wonderful, fantastic, uplifting, and all those things. But if only it were ORGANIZED it would have ended by 9:30! But who cares. The entire thing was done by kids, and run by kids, and they did a darn good job.

Journal Entry #63: Sunday, November 10

This Is One Politically Crazy Country!

Anyone who's following the political happenings over here may be aware that last week the whole government flip-flopped. I'll skip all the gory details and simply refer to the little "chess game" that Sharon and Netanyahu are playing. Sharon's move: offer Netanyahu position of foreign minister. Netanyahu's move: Sure, I'll take the job, IF...(and names his price of 'early elections') Sharon's move: Oh well, too bad – I'm not paying your price.

So then what happened? Aside from the whole Netanyahu thing, Sharon DID call for early elections. And Netanyahu stuck his pawn in front of Sharon's Queen and grabbed at the foreign minister post! (Please pardon my chess analogy if it makes no sense. I have NO IDEA how to play chess). So what does that leave us? A Prime Minister and a Foreign Minister who are mud-slinging, arch-enemies, running against each other in the upcoming elections. Just to give you an idea, imagine if Dick Cheney started whole-heartedly bashing George W.?

And We Got To See Where It All Happens

The third grade took a class trip today. Not my son's third grade. MY "third" grade in Ulpan. (The difference in OUR class trips is that the students do the driving and no one is allowed to bring a gun!) We went to the Knesset and to the Supreme Court. The Knesset is a very simple, yet beautiful building. It is filled with symbolism such as the layout of the Knesset members' seating is shaped like a menorah. Then we walked to the ten-year-old Supreme Court building which is truly special, incorporating several contrasts such as old and new, lines and circles, law and justice, I mean, uh, that's not supposed to be a contrast! Anyway, the tour guide was very nice, even though she did speak in a somewhat monotonous Hebrew that successfully put me to sleep once she had us all sitting.

We finished our tour several hours after the last bite of food went into my mouth, and the teacher suggested we go down to the (strictly kosher!) cafeteria for a quick bite. Sounds great! I quickly said, as I looked around and found no one agreeing. Well maybe just the people who rode with me in my car will be willing to stop for a few minutes. A quick poll resulted in four "not hungry, but don't mind if you stop" answers, and three "I'm an Arab and it's Ramadan so I'm fasting" answers. You guessed it. I closed my mouth and thought hungry thoughts until we finally reached my car and I devoured my apple.

Things Are Not Always What They Seem...

Speaking of fruit, ever see the famous prickly pear, or sabra fruit that grows here? It's quite bizarre looking, being a big cactus with leaf-shaped cactus protrusions that have the further protuberance of the fruit growing out of them. They are a challenge to handle and if you don't know what you are doing you can end up with a mouthful of prickles. If you're lucky enough to have an expert open it for you, you will enjoy a very delicious fruit. Anyway, I was wondering what the season is for sabra fruit. I don't know, but we do have a little sabra growing in our home, but we're not expecting it until some time in May...

Journal Entry #64: Tuesday, November 12

Computer Problems

As doctors' kids can get sick, computer professional's wives can screw up their computers. This computer professional's wife is no exception. For those of you who don't know, I brainlessly opened a worm attachment to my computer that *clearly stated* exactly what it was going to do once I downloaded it, but of course I never read the fine print! The end of the story is that my computer professional husband spent over an hour trying to undo the damage I caused, and I hope none of you received it as a result of my lack of brains.

Oh, and about my computer, it seems to be enjoying my journals so much, that it's been sending it out in duplicate. (Oh, you think that's my fault too? You're probably right. I'll ask my husband to fix the problem...)

Good Thing School Is Close By

My kids, or, I should say, one of my kids, tends to leave things home like her lunch. Being just a five minute drive, I'm able to deliver what she leaves often before she even realizes it is missing. To get into my daughters' gated school, I must first present myself at the guard booth with my reason for being there. Of course the reason is always in my hand, in the form of a lunchbox or a textbook, at which we share a brief chuckle at the frequency of items left at home and I make my delivery. The piece de resistance was when my daughter called me from school to tell me that her brand new boots had broken at the sole and could I bring her sneakers. When I showed up at the guard booth with a pair of *shoes,* that was just too much.

One Scary Ride

This morning Lawrence and I were driving to Ulpan like we always do, down that road that many people avoid yet is a part of our life. Shortly before a particular army roadblock (many of which are in places in Judea and Samaria to check for suspicious people and objects) there are often many Arabs milling about, crossing the street in one direction or another for it is a bus depot for them. As we were passing the Arabs, I saw something that made me scream at the top of my lungs and went into a panic. Lawrence, who was driving, looked horrified. He swerved briefly, his heart racing and franticly asked me what happened. Completely mortified and feeling terrible for scaring him out of his wits, I made the admission that there was a spider hanging from my hat, an inch away from my face. (Come on, wouldn't you have screamed??) I even made him stop at the roadblock so that I could get out and brush off every inch of me, mentally ridding myself of the possibility of a spider being anywhere on me. (I think it took Lawrence until we had reached Ulpan before he had completely calmed down.) Boy, did I ever feel bad!!

Journal Entry #65: Friday, November 15

This One Gets The Gold Star

If you have one, that is. My daughter's teacher likes to give out "gold stars" on papers they do well on. How do I know this? Because the gold *circle* on the top of Shira's test said "gold star" on it, in my daughter's writing. This was to let me know that it was what the teacher said it was or else I might not have recognized that it was a gold star. More important was that the next test, which had an unmistakable *green* circle stuck on it, had the words gold star or I certainly would have mistaken it for a lime, and that can't possibly be an indicator of a good test score. Why, I asked Shira, does your teacher feel the need to call every sticker she has a "gold star"? No idea, she responded. I suppose it's a language thing.

A Language Thing

I played hooky from Ulpan the other day to help my friend with a catering job she was doing. Besides from being a balloon blower-upper, tomato-slicer, and everything-taster, I also became the lasagna-server by default when I started to slice it and people suddenly lined up in front of me. This shouldn't be a problem, after all, how difficult is it to serve lasagna? Not difficult at all, until people start speaking to you in rapid-fire, slurred Hebrew. In fact, I realized the reason I understand everything in Ulpan, and hardly anything on the street. It's because when people know that you know hardly anything, they speak to you slowly, carefully, loudly (in case we're deaf?), without slang, and without slurring their words. When people see you serving lasagna, they assume you have enough brain to understand "I'm deathly allergic to eggplant, is there any in the lasagna?" Meanwhile, I think they're saying how delicious it looks and I smile and say, "Thank you." Several people walked away looking at me funny so I hope I didn't make any offensive remarks or insult someone's grandmother. I kind of reminded myself of my mother's Polish cleaning lady who used to "yes" you to death when she didn't have a clue what you were talking about.

My Amazing Discovery

Speaking of cleaning ladies, I have made an amazing discovery. It is amazing how my whole family seems to be working much harder at keeping the house clean than ever before. (Not that my house is spotless, just cleaner than it would have been!) I attribute it to the fact that for the first time in our spoiled lives, we don't have our cleaning lady to pick up after us. (Though I would do anything to get her here!) I've theorized that when you know without any doubt that you will have to clean up every mess you make, you simply make fewer messes.

Journal Entry #66: Sunday, November 17

A Very Sad Day

I assume by now you've all heard about the ambush in Hebron where 12 soldiers and police were killed and more than a dozen people injured, some critically. Here it has affected us very deeply where people from my own town lost family members, relatives or friends. Funeral processions went down the main road in Gush Etzion (where we live) and there were many army and police vehicles, and ordinary citizens on the streets showing support. My eldest daughter was among those people, having gone with her school. Had we known about it we would have gone as well.

Savor The Special Moments...

...For those times are what life is all about. I was relaxing in my candlelit living room last night, playing Beatles ballads on my guitar, when my daughters came up from downstairs to go to bed. Shortly after I said "Goodnight," and they were in their rooms, my 11-year-old, Lexi, came back out with her blanket, snuggled up on the couch near me, and fell asleep to my pathetic version of Eleanor Rigby. It was like a timeless escape from all reality. No stress, no time-constraints, only my fingers complaining when they had had enough.

At the end of the day, so to speak, it is important to be able to live, and enjoy, and do the things that are special and most meaningful with the ones you love. I think that in difficult times like these that is the most important advice I can give; At least to myself.

We should have only good news to share.

4

Learning...

Journal Entry #67: Tuesday, November 19

A World Of Contrast

Yesterday, the main road to Jerusalem was closed due to construction, so traffic was diverted through a friendly(?) Arab village called Wallja. As I drove through at a snail's pace due to traffic I was astonished to see, one after another, huge and beautiful mansions on the right side of the road. Modern and beautiful. Even more astonishing was the stark contrast right across the street. Not slums or a trailer park. We're talking BIG contrast. I mean ancient ruins; wild and untouched. So to my right I have clean, cultivated, rich, manicured, new and beautiful. To my left I have unkempt, mysterious, broken, old and fascinating. They should charge admission to drive through this place! This wasn't a *de*tour. It was a *tour*!

Very Precious Cargo

After several months of pretending it wasn't there, we've finally started to go through the many remaining boxes from our lift. Not even out of guilt. Just pure necessity. Anyway, as you may know, the majority of our stuff was packed by the movers. Though we have no idea what they put in what boxes, it was infinitely worth it for them to do it, because I'd probably still be packing if it had been left to me. In any case, they did a pretty good job at maximizing box space, and at wrapping and protecting delicate items. So we were going through one of the boxes and inside was a small (3"x6"?) packet that was very well wrapped in the blank newsprint they used and taped with their packing tape. However, it felt so light that for a moment I thought it was just paper, and why did the movers make this stupid packet, and I was ready to throw it out. But no, they couldn't have done something that dumb. There must be something in it. So I got a scissors, unwrapped several layers of nothing, until I finally reached the valuable treasure: A pair of plastic Delta wings that your kids get on the plane. You know something? If one of the moving men thought it was that valuable, I think I'm going to package it right back up again and send it to him!

Who Was That Masked Family?

Well, we finally did it! We all went for our brand new gas masks! Isn't that so exciting? Seriously though, don't all freak out now. Do you have smoke detectors in your homes? Does this mean you're expecting your neighbor to set your house on fire? Of course not. It just happens to be that our neighbor is Saddam Hussein and he's a certified psychopath. But the fact is that it is a precautionary thing that everyone here has, and the fact that we now have them does not make it any more or less likely that we will actually ever need them.

We got them at one of the malls here, where they have a room set up with all of the fitting equipment and teaching supplies. We purposely went on a day that the kids were home in the afternoon so that they could all be properly fitted even though our friends told us that wasn't necessary. What do they mean, it's not necessary? The nurse in me wondered. After all, I've been fitted many times for T.B. masks and I know all about microorganisms floating through the air and such. Of course they will need to be fitted.

They weren't fitted. They just gave us each our little sealed box, and sent us on our merry way. But wait! I stammered in my broken Hebrew, we don't even know what's inside the box or what to do with it all! Oh, came the helpful reply, here's a brochure. It's all in there.

I figured it was up to us. So I let the kids try on all the gas masks in the display. At least they touched and felt them and won't be afraid of them. G-d willing, we'll never need them, but if we do I guess we'll just wing it!

We left there with our six little packages and did the compulsory when-you're-in-the-mall-you-have-to-shop shopping. Got the girls some stuff, got Lawrence some stuff, but the boys had a valid complaint that can be summed up in Ezra's words: "The only thing you got us is gas masks!" I suppose it wouldn't help if we wrapped them in fancy paper and called them Chanukah presents?

Journal Entry #68: Thursday, November 21

First of all, I wanted to let everyone know that we are all fine and were nowhere near the bombing today. Of course there are dozens of families who were not so fortunate and it pains me to no end to hear of the continuous suffering and attacks. Many of you are so much more aware of what is happening in Israel now that you have a personal contact here. I apologize for the added stress of knowing someone so close to such a difficult conflict. Perhaps it will at least earn the benefit of extra prayers that may not have been said otherwise. I hope so!

The Heat Is On In Israel

...but it's not on in my house. Not by choice of course. Though it's been mostly pleasant during the day, the temperature has been dropping to 40 degrees or maybe lower at night. To me that's "turn on the heat" weather. So what's the problem? Well, we have no idea how to turn it on. There's this oven thing in our living room which is supposed to heat some water or something which then heats the radiators in the rooms. I'm sure I got that totally wrong, but one way or another, we have no clue how to turn it on, and if you remember anything I've ever said about my landlord, she's not the easiest person to deal with. We've been asking her several times a week for the past few weeks, and she keeps on saying she's coming and then doesn't show. At least we will have our heat by December 1st if not before, because she will certainly come for her rent check!

Oops! Ran Out Of Gas

But it was our clothes dryer that stalled. There are no gas lines where we live, so we buy these gas "balloons" (little tanks) which are placed outside, hooked to our stove and dryer. Then when we start running out, we call for a replacement. The system works perfectly IF you call when you're running low. Then the guy will come immediately, often on the same day, and replace the empty balloons. If you're like us, however, then you wait until the dryer is running cold and then the guy will certainly not be able to come for another week because when you REALLY need something, that's usually when it's not available. At least that's what happened this time. So, another week without doing any laundry. The irony of this story is that I had stayed home from Ulpan today just to give me a chance to catch up on it! (As I've said before, these are the things that make one *appreciate* doing laundry!!)

Our Ulpan Trip

Yesterday Lawrence and I joined the other students in our Ulpan for an all-day trip. We went to Ben-Gurion's home in Tel Aviv which is now a museum, and to a Biblical nature reserve near Modi'in called Neot Kedumim. But that's not what I'm writing about. I wanted to tell you about our arrival back in Jerusalem. First of all, we went by chartered bus. The driver nicely dropped people off at their bus stops if he happened to pass any of them.

But we were parked at the YMHA (Beit HaNoar) where the Ulpan is, so like half the bus, we waited for our arrival there. Finally, the bus driver stopped at a bus stop down the road and on the other side of the street from the Y. We all waited for those last people to get off so that we can get to the Y. Suddenly someone wondered out loud if maybe the driver intended for us to get off "here". Impossible, several others said. Why would he leave us here? One guy looked up and realized that the bus driver, himself, had gotten off the bus and we were all just sitting there. We found the bus driver and asked him. Looking at us like we had defective brains he told us quite unceremoniously that this was it and to get off. Surprised, Lawrence and I, and one other guy got off and started to walk. Meanwhile, the others were either too flabbergasted or too furious and started to argue with the bus driver. I don't know the end of the story because we left. But that was when our troubles started. The lot where we parked was so crammed with cars, that it took us a half hour and several screaming matches with irate Israelis (who really know how to scream!) before we got out. By the way, we were two of those irate Israelis. I thought Lawrence was going to punch someone at one point, and it was a *woman!*

Journal Entry #69: Sunday, November 24

They Call Chicago "The Windy City"?

They obviously haven't been to Neve Daniel. I'd like to buy a wind-speed measurer. Think there is such a thing? We'd don't have the Doppler weather report on the news every night with predicted wind direction and speed. (We don't even get the news!) We gauge it by having everyone in the family stand outside and checking to see who gets blown over and in what direction they fall. Seriously though, I was on the top of the mountain tonight, getting my mail, and my daughter and I were getting out on opposite sides of the car. As we opened our doors, one door blew open, and the opposite door blew shut. Small children are likely to blow away. Instead of weather reports, they should have a wind-rating system, similar to the movies ratings: "G" – for General population; "PG" – Parents or Guardians to hold children's hands; "PG-13" – Parents guard your children under 13 carefully! "R" – Restricted to those over 150lbs. "X" – for X-tra large adults only!

Guard Duty

Another thing we don't have here is Wackenhut. For those of you unaccustomed to the lovely gated life of Boca Raton, it is a security service made up of very qualified people who don't even need a college degree to get their jobs. In our gated community the security service is a little different. But first, the similarities: you don't need a college degree for this job either. There you have it, the similarities! Here the job is actually an obligatory volunteer job. (Kind of an oxymoron, I know). You can get paid if someone badly doesn't want to do it and sells you his time slot. Otherwise you just do your time. Anyway, it's kind of like the citizen's observer patrol that many American communities have. Drive around your neighborhood in a souped up vehicle looking for suspicious characters. Except that here you get to carry a BIG gun. Believe it or not I once joined the Citizen's Observer Patrol in Boca Raton. I thought it was a great idea. It would have been if I'd joined with a friend. Instead I got to ride around for three hours with a guy who was at least a hundred years old. He drove. I slept. We didn't catch too many bad guys that night. (And then I quietly resigned). Lawrence has not been called to his volunteer duty yet, but he is out for the first time tonight with our friend, to keep him company and learn the ropes. Not to mention, help the time pass for our friend!

Journal Entry #70: Monday, November 25

The Delights Of Insurance Claims In Israel

Remember our totaled car that they didn't total? And remember that we had the brilliance to get direct car insurance, instead of through an agent, since it was significantly cheaper? What did this do for us? It gave us the opportunity of a lifetime to do what insurance agents do. Without training, without the language, and with a system that is totally foreign to us. Actually, it is a system that is totally foreign to anyone with half a brain. One thing about my husband is he is extremely thorough. He dove into the whole process headfirst and thoroughly researched what needed to be done. In fact he was so involved that at first it seemed that it would be no big deal. It was simply a matter of getting together all of the paperwork that they needed and sending it in. That much is true. The *difficult* part is actually getting them to tell you exactly what paperwork they need! Lawrence promptly sent in every single thing they had asked for, called to check that they'd received it and that all was well, and found out that they'd forgotten to ask for one little thing. No big deal, right? Except that it has happened now at least half a dozen times and more than a month after the accident they are still coming up with "just one more thing" that they need! It's almost hilarious except for the fact that American Express is expecting more than $9,000 from us, and the other guy's insurance is never going to pay until our insurance is satisfied that they have every piece of paperwork that has ever existed. For example, they asked us to get a form from the bank. My husband went on a wild goose chase to procure this form that our bank told us *does not even exist.* You would think they were stalling, except they're not even the ones expected to pay!

A Heated Attempt

Remember that oven thing that's supposed to heat our house? Well yesterday Lawrence decided to try and turn the thing on himself. After all, it's simply lighting a pilot light. What could be so hard? With my son, Eitan, closely observing, he threw a little match into the furnace. He ended up with a rip-roaring fire! My son took one look at the inferno and exclaimed, "Should we run, Abba?!" as he stood at the door ready to bolt. Luckily there was never a safety issue as it was all contained, though my husband quickly extinguished the darn thing and decided to wait until another day.

Another Day

Today, Lawrence did all his thorough research on strange, Israeli, heating furnaces. I had nothing to do with it, but the end result is that we have a cute, little fire in the furnace now, and the house no longer feels like a refrigerator.

Journal Entry #71: Tuesday, November 26

An Even Better Car-fixing Story

And this one isn't even ours. Our friends in Ramot had their car broken into and took their car to have a smashed-in window replaced. When they picked up the car, it seemed that they hadn't even cleaned the window properly after installing it. Our friend started to clean it himself and discovered that it wasn't dirt at all, but scratches. They replaced his window with an old, used window! He brought it back and complained, and they innocently explained that it was a "temporary window." Yeah, right. It's permanent unless you figure them out! I guess there are crooked car-repair shops everywhere.

On The Brighter Side...Large Gathering #1

Last night I took the girls to a concert in Efrat. It was a performance of Neshama Carlebach, an American, who is the daughter of the late Shlomo Carlebach, a Jewish music legend. She came to sing and perform for the women of Gush Etzion and, specifically, to support Kever Rachel and the women's group from Gush Etzion who go there weekly. The music was wonderful and the spirit was very lively. People spontaneously got up and danced. What was especially meaningful was here was a woman who has been dedicating concert after concert to the people of Israel and here she was performing for those very people she has been dedicating her past concerts to. And we were those people.

Large Gathering #2

Today we went to a rally that was organized with a similar tone. Jews, and even some Christians, from the U.S. and some other countries, came on a number of simultaneous solidarity missions to show support for Israel. We were actually of a very small number of *Israelis* attending the rally, and who marched along with them through the Old City of Jerusalem. As we all gathered in the square in the Jewish Quarter and people of every stripe spontaneously got up to dance to a wonderful Israeli band, it struck me how this event was the flip-side of last night's. There, an American was performing for Israelis to show support. Here the Americans were at a performance of Israelis to show support. And there we were, in sort of a dual role, as the supporters and the supported.

Support Israel!

Quite honestly, both events were incredible, uplifting experiences. If I had to vote for a favorite, it would be today's, but there were some major bonuses today. First of all, my whole family was there. Not just the girls. Secondly, Boca Raton, the community we just moved from, sent their own youth mission and we were able to really see the event, not only through our own eyes as new Israelis, but through theirs, a group of people to whom we remain close, and from whom we have only recently departed.

Journal Entry #72: Thursday, November 28

In Search Of The Best Pizza

Anticipating the whole group of teenagers from Boca Raton over for lunch today, we tried to come up with the best place to get pizza, that wasn't too far away. The two local places that we know of are not our favorites. We entertained the crazy thought of bringing pizza back from Jerusalem and decided that lousy pizza was better than cold pizza and nixed that idea. Then our friend suggested the pizza from Beitar Illit, the next town over, which she highly recommended. Great idea! So I looked up the number in the Yellow Pages (we have those here too), and we went to Ulpan and planned on ordering from there. Which would have been fine except that the number didn't work. Feeling a bit panicky since you can't just arrive at a pizza shop and expect eight pies on the spot, I tried calling information (yup, we have that too!) and got a different number. And it worked! So I made the order and then asked the guy for directions. I stopped him when he said: "...the first pizza shop that you get to."

"Oh," I said in surprise. "Is there more than one in town?"

"Yes, there are two," he answered. "How did you hear about MY place?"

"Well actually," I admitted, "we heard that there was great pizza in your town. But I have no idea which place they were referring to." (Did you ever meet anyone as stupidly blunt as me?)

Poor guy. We went to pick up the pizza and he said only eight or nine times: "I hope you like the pizza" and "I hope the pizza is good." Well the pizza was very good. I better remember to call and tell him!

Eating The Pizza

The lunch worked out wonderfully. We were thrilled to have had the opportunity to host the teens from Boca. It was great to show them Neve Daniel, and we were glad to give them a clue as to why we ever left Boca Raton. After lunch my girls walked all of the kids down to the basketball court where they played a bit. It was really very special for Shira and Lexi and for us. And hopefully for our guests as well. It wasn't just "eating pizza."

Journal Entry #73: Sunday, December 1

Today's Event

Today we went to the holy city of Jerusalem to attend something that we have waited a whole year for. We went to see the second Harry Potter movie! Some might think I should be embarrassed to put it in such a way, but quite honestly I've been counting down the days and I was thrilled to see it! As far as the movie goes, it was at least as good as the last one though there were many omissions from the book, and actually some changes and additions. As far as the viewing goes, well that's another thing altogether.

The Viewing

First of all, state-of-the-art it wasn't. Actually, I was a bit surprised since we watched it at the brand new theater in the brand new Jerusalem mall. Boy were we spoiled at our beautiful, 20-theater multiplex with stadium seating in Boca Raton. This, too, is a multiplex, but that is where the similarities end. Each theater is tiny, with *one aisle only* (meaning if you're not at the aisle, then you're between the aisle and a wall.) The incline is so slight that I don't quite know why they bothered. The seats were comfortable enough, and surprisingly we were all able to see over the heads of the people in front of us. The movie started and all was fine except that I don't think anyone ever taught Israelis movie etiquette, like shutting cell phones during the show, and not talking. All this worked out very well for me since Ezra was asking me questions non-stop throughout the movie, and I didn't have to feel so bad about it.

Journal Entry #74: Monday, December 2

It's All In The Accent

My daughter's friend, Aviva, who is American-born but grew up in Israel, was over today looking at pictures of my (long-ago) trip to Europe. They got to the Amsterdam page and Lexi and I pointed out the pictures of Anne Frank's house and the secret annex. Her friend looked at us blankly having no clue who we were talking about. You know, I said encouragingly, the Diary of Anne Frank. But she still had no clue. How could this be? The Jewish state doesn't teach one of the most translated books of Jewish literature in this century? I decided to try one more approach:

"Did you ever hear of *Ahnna Frrrrrrrahnk?"* I asked Aviva in the best Israeli accent I could muster.

"Ohhhh, *Ahnna Frrrrrrrahnk.* Why didn't you say so in the first place?"

Journal Entry #75: Wednesday, December 4

Not The Israel You See On The News

This is what I told our guide today as Shira and I rode down a beautiful, almost deserted, stretch of beach between rock cliffs and the Mediterranean Sea at sunset on horseback. I'm not sure if he understood what I was talking about but I knew you all would. What an incredible feeling it was sitting high on a beautiful chestnut horse, feeling the ocean breeze, watching the sun begin its beautiful descent across the western sky, and experiencing this with my daughter, no less. It was exhilarating. Arriving back at the Netanya ranch that we set out from, I found my other three kids with Lawrence no less excited about the wonderful time they had had. Making their way down the cliffs, romping on the beach, getting wet (in December? Are they nuts?) and watching the same glorious sunset. This is our Israel, everyone! (And for the price of an El Al ticket, it can be yours as well!)

Horseback riding - exhilarating

Journal Entry #76: Thursday, December 5

The Trip That Didn't Happen (Yet)

After much talk and little action, today was to be the day that we finally would go to *Me'Arat Hamachpeilah* (The Cave of the Patriarchs) in Hebron. As one of the holiest graves in the world, and being that it's down the road from where we live, it certainly took us long enough to get our act together and plan the trip. We planned this trip with our friends Josh and Batsheva who live around 20 minutes away. We organized with the special tour bus that makes several weekly trips to the site that we would be picked up at the bus stop right outside Neve Daniel since it passes by anyway. We made sure they would have room for all eleven of us, and that it would not be a problem for the bus to make the extra stop at Neve Daniel. With everything set, our friends arrived here and we all took our food, drinks and *siddurim* (prayer books) and Lawrence dropped us off at the bus stop, then went to park. We came early since we weren't exactly sure how long it would take for the bus to get there from Jerusalem, and we didn't want to risk missing it.

The kids had a lovely time playing at the bus stop, and it's a good thing, because that's about all they did today. After we had waited for more than a half hour, we started to wonder if the bus would come at all. We almost hailed a passing bus until we saw "Ramallah" in bright letters on the side of it. Truth is it was probably going to Hebron as well, but we wouldn't have been very comfortable!

Finally we decided to give it five more minutes and then forget it. We looked in the distance and saw not one but two buses coming around the bend. The first one was a city bus, and the second one – It was our bus!! Joyful, we all stood up ready to hail it just in case the driver didn't remember to stop. Problem was, when buses are whizzing by at 65+ mph, how do you indicate to the first bus that *normally* stops where you are standing, that you *don't* want him, but that you *do* want the bus behind him who is tailgating so close that he can't see you anyway. You guessed it. The city bus stopped and the Hebron bus flew by. WAIT!!! We all screamed at the top of our lungs, arms waving, but to no avail. Meanwhile, the city bus was stopped, and they were looking at us like we were nuts.

Oh well. I had a lot of laundry to do anyway. I guess we'll go to Me'arat Hamachpeilah some other time. But you can't say we didn't try!

Journal Entry #77: Monday, December 9

Taking Hebrew To The Next Level

Okay, the impossible has happened. I have been promoted to the highest regular Hebrew Ulpan class known to mankind, level 6. It was purely by accident, I can assure you. We'll see how long it takes until they figure out that I can't speak Hebrew. The one person who is quite displeased with my placement is the teacher I had in level 4-5. Remember that two months into that three month class I decided that I couldn't take another day of it and demoted myself to level 3 just to get out of it. Now, one month later, all of the classes are starting fresh. Level 3 was quite easy even at the end. And level 4-5 had nothing new to interest me with. I spoke to the school director and she told me to go to 6. So I did.

Today, the second day into the new session, I bumped into my old 4-5 teacher. With her sugary smile she asked me what class I was in now (read between the lines: Where the heck could you possibly be if you just completed 3 and you're not in my class?) I proudly told her that I was in 6. But she just stared at me expectantly as if I were supposed to explain. So I added that the director had recommended that I go into 6, and besides, I had already been in 3, and in 4-5. She looked at me and icily told me that I had not "learned" 4-5, implying that I had hardly been there. I reminded her that I had been there for two thirds of the course, then I caught myself before I added that I left because I'd rather struggle in a class three times as hard before going back into that class.

But What Are They Saying?!

So now I'm in level 6. There is something entirely strange about Hebrew in this country. Here I am, in what's supposed to be this high level Hebrew class. (I've heard it referred to as the "college professor" level). So far I have understood pretty much everything that the teacher has said. That should indicate a fairly competent ability in Hebrew, wouldn't you think? Then why is it that as soon as I go anywhere else and someone starts to speak Hebrew, I haven't a *clue* as to what they're saying! It seems that Israelis have some universal slang and syllable-swallowing that only they themselves understand. After I complete Ulpan I suppose I will have to go to a finishing school to learn to actually *talk* like the Israelis, and then perhaps I'll begin to understand them. In the meantime, it would help if I could learn to form a proper grammatical sentence in Hebrew.

Journal Entry #78: Thursday, December 12

Foreign Food

Yesterday my son brought a strange and unusual food to school for lunch. Back where we come from, it's known as *macaroni and cheese.* But as far as Eitan's classmates were concerned, he could have just as easily brought in fried slugs. "Eeeeewwwww!" they politely intoned upon viewing his delectable edibles. They all inspected his food as if it were a specimen of sorts, until an astute child in his class pronounced, "Oh! It's spaghetti!" Mystery solved.

More Foreign Food

Yesterday we went to lunch with our friends to a German restaurant that had been transplanted to Israel from Switzerland but actually reminded me of New York. They boast 200+ years in the deli and sausage business, and from what they served us, I believe it! After an exciting array of sausages and patés, I was perfectly delighted to eat a good, old hot pastrami sandwich. This may not sound very exciting, but believe me – it is. I didn't even know that pastrami existed in Israel. It even had good mustard! In my condition, this may have to be a weekly event.

Level 6

I have now completed a full week in level 6 at Ulpan. What do I have to say about it? I love it!! The teachers are wonderful and the subject material is both interesting and challenging enough to keep me attentive. The amazing thing? I don't want to be late, and I don't want to miss a day for anything! Besides that I would be hopelessly lost if I missed, I simply don't want to miss anything. I really like the class. I don't know if anyone is as astonished about this as I am. It certainly was a pleasant surprise!

First Job Interview

Lawrence got a great job interview through a neighbor at one of the big hospitals in Jerusalem. The first interview went very well, and in fact he was called back for a second interview. Wow, imagine moving to Israel and getting a job from the first interview you land! Sounds too good to be true!! Yeah, well, unfortunately it is. Oh, well. The second interview went very nicely too. We were left waiting for several weeks while they decided between Lawrence and two other candidates who both had somewhat inferior experience to his. After quite some time they finally dropped the verdict. NO. They told him that his experience was certainly the best, but they really wanted someone who was proficient in Hebrew. Oh well. Now don't go feeling all bad for us because we're not feeling bad at all. When the right job comes, it will come.

Journal Entry #79: Saturday, December 14

Who Said That Kids Learn Languages Easily???

Whoever said that obviously forgot to tell MY kids. Someone was even so bold as to say, "If you make aliyah in the summer, your kids will be fluent by Chanukah." Oh yeah? Maybe Chanukah of a different year! Of my four kids, two are starting to get it (emphasize the *starting*), and the other two? Well, they may read this, so I'll just leave it at that. And by the way, it has NOTHING to do with age, for the two having difficulty are one of the older two kids and one of the younger two kids. We've been doing what we can to get extra help. They have a few hours a week of private Hebrew lessons in school; they have workbooks to do during the more difficult lessons, etc. But it really isn't much in the whole scheme of things. The majority of their day is spent in lessons they largely don't understand. Though they may come to understand it eventually, it isn't the fastest, most efficient way to learn a language. Also, they all have friends who speak English. That is a major advantage and disadvantage rolled into one. On the one hand it gives them badly needed social support. On the other hand, it doesn't force them to speak Hebrew. So, we've been on somewhat of a quest to find out ways to really help them with the Hebrew.

The Big "Secret"

There is Ulpan for children in Israel. That is the big secret. How do we know it's a secret? Well, because no one told us about it, so it must be. But we foiled "them"! It is actually quite amazing how we found out. In speaking to friends in Beit Shemesh, I found out that their kids are getting Ulpan right in their neighborhood. Meanwhile, my kids get a few hours a week and just sit through classes that they don't understand the rest of the time. I briefly considered driving them to Beit Shemesh every day, but thought that there must be a better way. A few days later, I had a meeting with the advisor for Ezra's school. I mentioned, in passing, the language issues we were having with our other kids and how I had found out about the Ulpan in Beit Shemesh. The next day she called me and told something unbelievable. On the bus that morning she started a conversation with a girl she'd never met, who just *happened* to have made aliyah on *our plane*, and who just *happened* to be in an Ulpan for teens in Jerusalem!!

Of course, I don't believe in coincidences. I immediately called the girl's mother and got the information I needed. I brought my daughters to the school, for really it is a full-fledged school that bases its entire curriculum on teaching Hebrew. My girls were tested for placement, and I tentatively planned on starting them on Sunday. There was one catch: I didn't want them to abandon the friends and the environment of the new school that they have finally become comfortable with. I called their principal and ran my idea by him: that they would go to the Ulpan in the morning and then finish their day in their regular classes. I voiced my concerns that it may be intrusive to the class to come so late every day. He agreed. It would be intrusive. But nonetheless, he thought it was the best idea yet, and barring any objections from the teachers, I should go ahead with it. Yippee!! They start tomorrow!

Journal Entry #80: Tuesday, December 17

Everyone Has Their Limits

Our Ulpan teacher gave us a test today that nobody knew about, and I probably would have failed even if I did know. This is much too reminiscent of high school. I was so stressed while taking it, that I couldn't believe a stupid piece of paper could elicit so much anxiety. Well, it wasn't the paper. It was all those little blanks to fill in, and all I could do was draw a blank!

In the end she felt bad since no one was prepared, and everyone complained. We simply went over it in class. But the stress had already happened. All I could think of while I sat at my desk staring at the thing was, what do I need this for? I'm a pregnant mother (there, for all those of you who've missed the hints!!) with millions of responsibilities and things to do. I don't want to take tests!!! Okay, now I feel better. After we reviewed the test, the teacher asked me if I now remembered a particular answer she had just given. To her surprise I said, "No." I then added, "I'm sure it's in here," and pointed to my head, "but I don't know where!"

The Ulpan For Kids

Our girls have now spent three days at their Ulpan. We are very happy. They started in the same level but one of them may move up. It is a similar system to our Ulpan, with homework, and, I imagine, tests too. But they're used to tests. Hopefully they won't get all stressed out like their mother!! There is also art and music. The timing is great. They are able to get a ride into school with us in the morning and then they take the bus home in the afternoon. They are thrilled because of two things: We let them take the bus, and we let them carry our cell phone every day. They've made friends right away which is key to their adjustment there. In fact they went to one of their friend's homes straight from school today. Oh yeah, about that...

The Girls' Adventure After School

First of all, their friend lives in Kiryat Arba. As in the next town over from Hebron. They went to their friend's house with the plan to go swimming with her at the indoor pool there. This was fine, except that when they called to finalize their plan, I wasn't home. Lawrence knew we had decided it was okay, but he didn't know that we had never made a detailed arrangement, such as when and how they would get home. This was a minor detail, made into a bigger problem, when we realized they had left their cell phone at the girl's house. When we finally tracked them down, after numerous phone calls and finally actually calling the pool, they were surprised to find out that they needed to leave. Immediately. They asked us if we could pick them up there. I sheepishly explained that though Kiryat Arba is on the same road that we drive everyday, it is in an area that I am unfamiliar with and am not comfortable driving to. And certainly not at night for the first time. So they are now on their way to the bus after having hitched rides to and from the pool with their friend. Next time my kids go anywhere I will be sure to get a detailed itinerary of their every move – and cross out everything that I don't like!!

Journal Entry #81: Wednesday, December 18

If It's Empty, Fill It Up

A sage bit of advice. Next time we will heed it. Last night Lawrence, Lexi and I went to Beit Shemesh for a Bar Mitzvah. It is a little known fact that Beit Shemesh is actually very close to Gush Etzion for those who are willing to drive on the roads that we drive on every day anyway. (And for all others, we might as well live in China.) At any rate, the road is quite lovely on a nice day; winding through mountains and valleys, scenic countryside and occasional villages dotting the landscape. Again, that is by *day.* At *night,* however, especially when it's a bit on the rainy and foggy side, the winding through mountains serves as nothing more than winding our stomachs in knots and our nerves into taut balls of twine. But, no matter, we happily rode off to Beit Shemesh and not only had a lovely time at the Bar Mitzvah, but even managed a late visit with friends who were in from Boca Raton. We left at 11:00, they wished us a safe drive, and we were off.

We knew that we were low on gas, but there always seemed to be enough. There was no gas station nearby, but we would be passing a few so we weren't worried. We should have been. We turned onto the narrow, winding road and started to climb through the mountainous forest when putt – putt – putt – sputter – kaput. Our car ran out of gas – in the middle of nowhere – in the middle of the night – on a road without streetlights, and very little traffic. We debated putting on our hazard lights. Lawrence said the noise irritated him. But maybe he didn't want to announce to all the unsavory characters that might pass us that "Look at us! We're sitting ducks!" I know the thought crossed my mind.

We called our friend Raffi, who, without hesitating, grabbed an empty gas can, and drove out to help us. Of course he was a half hour away, and still had to stop and buy us gas.

We settled back and tried to relax when a car that had just passed us turned on his reverse lights and pulled up alongside us. Instantly on the alert, we checked him out through our closed window. Turns out it was in American guy named Benny who lives in Beitar. He wanted to know if everything was alright, and if there was anything he could do. We thanked him profusely for daring to stop, and told him our friend was on the way. Let me tell you, this man who stopped is a rare breed indeed. He felt that it would take very long for the gas to get here, and though he could have gone home with a clear conscience and a great feeling for even stopping, he decided to go get gas for us on the chance that our wait would be those few minutes shorter. He had to borrow a gas can from the service station he went to and then go back there to return it. He wouldn't even take money for the gas.

Of course our friend Raffi showed up just after we finished pouring in Benny's can of gas. We felt bad having had him shlep all the way out for nothing, but how could we have known? As Raffi put it, "That's what friends are for."

Journal Entry #82: Thursday, December 19

Anyone See The Neve Daniel Weather Report?

No? Well maybe that's because there is no such thing. Which is really a shame since we have a weather system all our own and the only way to know the weather here is to step outside and look around. I've looked on the Weather Channel website and found temperatures in Jerusalem, which is ten minutes north of here, of 66; in Hebron, which is twenty minutes south of here, of 66, yet somehow our Brookstone thermometer registers a nippy 45. Quite honestly, I wouldn't be surprised to find that Tel Aviv registered 66 as well. I think that those weather people can't imagine that a tiny country like ours can have so many different weather events going on, so they just take Tel Aviv's weather and attach it to all the other cities. In fact when it showed a current temperature reading of "66", it also said, "low of 42, high of 54". So I don't know why they bother!

What's interesting about that is that even if the Jerusalem forecast were accurate, it wouldn't help us much. We seem to exist in our own private little weather system. I was actually somewhat of a "Weather Channel" junkie in the states. If I knew there was a hurricane brewing out next to Africa, I would watch it until it was absolutely, positively not going to hit Florida. (Which would take a week or two I might add). Major contrast to Neve Daniel. How do I know if there's a hurricane? I get one of those baseball-pitch-speed-measuring devices and measure the flying objects during a rain storm. Actually, if you know the right people you can get weather tips and hints. Like, I've heard a rumor that we will be getting snow in the next 24 hours. Of course it will only be newsworthy if it hits a major city. But you'll hear about it from me! I've also heard that we will be getting winds tonight that will exceed 100 km per hour. In fact we were warned to anchor down our CARS. Can you imagine? Now where do they get their information??

Quality Time In The Morning

And I didn't spend it in Ulpan. Ezra had an appointment in Jerusalem so that was a great excuse not to go to Ulpan at all. Ezra and I had a blast walking through the center of town today, despite the cold and rain. Hot chocolate on Ben Yehuda, strolling into quaint shops, exploring the little streets. It was a lot of fun. I guess on Sunday it will be back to Ulpan, but every once in a while one needs a break.

Journal Entry #83: Friday, December 20, Part A

Neighborly Warnings

With the approach of very heavy wind, I may not have the local meteorologist to give me a weather report, but I do have lots of nice neighbors. As I referenced earlier, a kindly man came over to warn me that I had better place heavy boulders at each tire so that my 9-passenger mini-van doesn't, well I'm not exactly sure what he thought might happen to it. Surely he doesn't think it will blow away? Another neighbor warned me to be extra careful when opening car doors in the intense wind. It has happened before, she reported, that the wind added so much force to the out-swinging car door that it blew right off its hinges. People have also been speculating whether our little grocery store, which looks like it's been pasted together out of cardboard and is in the unlucky location of right on top of the hill where the wind is strongest, will be able to hold up to the extreme wind.

My Own Private Weather "Channel"

Hey, I've got eyes and ears, don't I? And right now my ears are hearing whistling, trees and other objects knocking together, sudden large gusts that intensify the volume (No volume button here. Perhaps that's why I'm up at 3:25 AM?) Some glass tinkling, windows clattering, our smokestack whining and moaning. Basically it sounds like the big, bad wolf is outside huffing and puffing to blow our house in. As for what I see? Well, to be honest I don't want to get too close to any windows because earlier a window that Lawrence had put so much effort into fixing so that it would seal tight (He actually put on goggles and took out some sort of a guy-tool and made zillions of sparks fly off of the steel frame. My kids loved it!) actually blasted open in the wind. (Our windows are all double-doored that open inwards.) I imagine that it wouldn't have felt too good if I had been enjoying the view out of that very window when it happened. But I do see various odd displaced objects like a big empty garbage bag in our garden. Of course the trees are swaying out of control. It's really quite astonishing.

More News Than I Even Expected

Our community puts out a weekly bulletin with all of the announcements and such. It is generally several pages long, and all in Hebrew of course. This makes for quite a tedious affair if we actually want to know what's happening around here. Being as news starved as I am, I decided to try to read it and see if I could find even a little blurb about the impending weather. I had almost finished and thought it wouldn't be mentioned at all, when I glanced at a letter on the last page and discovered it to be a FULL PAGE of information on what to do in case of snow, written by the Neve Daniel Snow Committee, or something. Can you imagine? It included things like, If you have a snow related problem, DO NOT CALL THE ARMY, and If plowing is necessary, ONLY THE TOP ROAD WILL BE PLOWED. Therefore, if you will be needing to drive anywhere, park your car on the top road. (We live on the second-to-bottom road). What I still don't know is if the letter was printed in specific anticipation for this weekend, or if it was only a general letter for the winter season. I guess I'll find out this weekend on My Own Private Weather Channel.

T.G.I.F.

We look forward to hunkering down this weekend with tea, hot cocoa, and hopefully some good novels. Stay tuned for the on-location report!

Journal Entry #84: Friday, December 20, Part B

More Lovely House Stories

Now that we've got a front door leak fairly under control, it was high time for a new problem to crop up. And it did! With all of the heavy wind and rain, we found the rest of the spots in our house that are susceptible to leakage. All of our windows! And I don't mean little drips, here. We're talking big puddles and minor flooding on the floor. We defended ourselves, from this little breach in our comfort, by placing towels in front of all the guilty windows and wringing them out periodically. It was especially yucky when one approached one of the windows in socks and stepped unsuspectingly into a cold, invading puddle. Then, we would make more soggy towels by placing clean ones on the floor. (And make lots of extra laundry!)

A Little Window On Our Life

Eitan pointed at one of the windows in our house and said, "What kind of proof is this?"

"Proof of what?" I asked, thinking he was pointing outside and wanting "proof" that it would snow or something.

"No," he corrected me. "I mean like 'break-proof', 'rock-proof', 'bullet-proof'?"

"Oh," I nodded in understanding, acutely aware of the commentary his question makes on life here. Then I added, "Actually, the window is 'nothing-proof'. It doesn't even keep out the rain!!"

Journal Entry #85: Saturday, December 21

Weekend Forecast: Cozy Shabbos Indoors Reading Good Novels

NOT!! Well it all started out fine. I braved the freezing rain and blustery wind to go and stock up on supplies for the weekend: Milk, fresh bread, cappuccino mix, and takeout food. I put up a homemade chicken soup for Friday night, and made a big, yummy *chulent* (Shabbos stew) to simmer all night and have hot for Shabbos lunch. I even braved the elements to walk over to a not-very-close neighbor to get a large supply of books to hold us over through Shabbos and beyond. We were ready. We were prepared. We were fortified! Friday night was fine. We all enjoyed bowls of piping hot chicken soup and watched the outdoor thermometer as it slowly edged its way down to that magic number – 32 degrees. Magic, of course, because it could turn the rain into snow; at least according to our amateur calculations. We snuggled up on the couches after dinner and had hot tea, read our books and listened to the wind howl as we occasionally watched little hail pellets slide down the (leaky) window. We all went to sleep dreaming of snow.

A Few Minor Problems

The kids woke us at 8 a.m. to report that the electricity was off upstairs. Thinking right away of my poor chulent that should be bubbling away in the electric crock pot, I told them to quickly put the crock on the big oven-thing that warms our house, since it does not run on electricity, but on kerosene. I wasn't even sure if I was allowed to do that (laws of cooking on Shabbat) but I felt that we'll stick it on there now and ask questions later. At least if we did that we'd still have a chance to eat it. But all my hasty decision making was for nothing. Because, they then reported to us, the heater was off as well.

Come to think of it, I was feeling pretty cold. Lawrence checked the radiators in our room and they were completely cool. The heater had apparently been off for hours. Ditto the crock pot, and my hot water urn. Not only were we in a cold house, not only did we have nothing hot for lunch, but I didn't even have hot water to make coffee! Now THAT was an emergency! I put clothes on over my pajamas and went out in the yucky weather, with an empty thermos, to my neighbor, Judy, for hot water. I ended up staying for over an hour having coffee, pastries and conversation. But one of the best parts of the conversation was when she offered for us to stay for lunch and even crash at their house for the day so we could stay warm.

I went home to put on respectable clothes and gathered up my cold clan just in time for – SNOW!!! Now, you northerners may scoff at us; If it even lasted twenty minutes that was a lot. But, it was absolutely, positively snowing. Boy, did I have some happy kids!! They were ready to make snowballs and build snowmen. I didn't have the heart to explain that if you can't even make a footprint in it, it will be hard to make as much as a snow pebble. But they figured it out for themselves. No matter. Nothing could put a damper on them at that point.

We had lunch with Judy, Howie and their family and then I camped out on their couch all day. After Shabbat, Lawrence called our landlady to tell her our problems with the heat and the windows. The windows she promised to "silicon" for us on Wednesday and the heat she said she would tell her husband about. Sure enough, about 1 ½ hours later he showed up at our door! Turns out that the electricity did have something to do with the heat going off. But don't ask me to explain it, because I will sound much stupider if I try than if I just say nothing altogether. Oh, and we mentioned the badly leaking windows. His answer? "Yeah, that's what happens when it storms."

"So what did you do about it?" I wondered in disbelief.

"Same as you. Towels." At least we have our heat back on.

Journal Entry #86: Monday, December 23

Mission Accomplished

Coming from Florida, there were a lot of essential pieces missing from our wardrobes. One of those things was boots. Not that you can't get by without them, but we live in the Vermont of Israel. If there is snow anywhere, we will be snowed in. Even if it's just rain, the cold and wind added to it makes a great case for having a pair of toasty warm boots to keep your feet nice and dry. Except that we couldn't find anything that was both appealing AND reasonably priced. You may have heard the story about the only boots we did get, for Shira, which lost a sole on the first day of wear. So we can add quality to our list of boot requirements. Anyway, I took the girls to Jerusalem yesterday, and with much time to spare on the meter, we managed to get boots for Lexi and me, and the assurance from the salesman that if we brought him Shira's boots, he would do what he could to get them fixed.

'Tis the Season

We were rather surprised driving home through Talpiot last night. The drive takes us partially down the road that leads to Bethlehem. They had a whole Christmas-light thing going on down a big portion of the road. We actually knew it was there, as we had seen it during the day, but somehow, lights look a heck of a lot different when they are lit up at night than when they are merely strings draped across the road, as during the day. The surprise was simply due to the fact that December in Israel is not synonymous with holiday lights and evergreen trees. We certainly live amongst a multitude of religions, and I have every respect for people practicing what they believe in. However, as a Jew, in the Jewish homeland, I really appreciate that the month of December does not obligate me to experience Christmas everywhere I turn.

Jerusalem Dummies

I mean of the mannequin variety. One storefront window reminded me as to why we are here. (Not that I need reminders). In America I've known Orthodox Jews who, embarrassed to be different, took off their yarmulkes when they went into stores. In this particular store, as in every place in Israel, no one feels different or out of place looking Jewish. But this store especially: there were yarmulkes on the mannequins!

Journal Entry #87: Wednesday, December 25

Tour Guides For The Day

A couple from Boca Raton, here for two weeks, wanted to see Gush Etzion. They contacted us, and we called the Regional Council right away

2nd Temple period mikvah on Derech Avot

to arrange something. Problem was that there was not much they could do for two or three tourists at a time. Well, there was no way we would allow people who wanted to see Gush Etzion to miss out simply because there was no organized tour to take them. Thus was created "Ben-David & Ben-David, Famous Tour Guides of Gush Etzion." (Famous only now, that all of YOU know about us!) Even our car played a nice role: with seating for *nine* we might as well put it to work! Of course we don't take money, but a generous donation towards your Gush Etzion charity-of-choice would be nice.

It was very enjoyable. Among other places, we took them to the Audio-Visual presentation (which we opted out of watching, having seen it three times in the past year!), then to the famous tree that provided Gush Etzion with its logo. We took them on *Derech Avot*, the Path of the Patriarchs, which is likely the route that Abraham took Isaac on the way to what became known as the Binding of Isaac, and has physical remnants from Temple times. We rounded out the tour by taking them to a most current and uplifting location, the Yeshiva of Gush Etzion, where high on the top of the mountain of Alon Shvut is nestled a beautiful, modern *Beit Medrash* or House of Learning, where at any given time, dozens, if not many more, are immersed in the study of Torah. Last, but not least, of course we took them to Neve Daniel for a visit to our own (rented, leaky) home.

Not All Bargains Are Worth The Money

Such is the case with the idiotic toaster we bought in New York at a store that sells 220 volt appliances before we came. May I point out that if there is no sample of an item in the store, it is for a good reason. Such is the lesson we learned – but at the expense of many slices of burnt toast. Apparently, our toaster is of the nostalgic variety. And I'm not referring to "classic good-looks". You see, in 1919 a design for toasters was patented which made it unnecessary to *watch* the toast to keep it from burning. By 1926 they were relatively foolproof. (Don't ask me where I got my information.) 1926. That was a long time ago. Toaster technology has come a long way since then. *So why in the world does my toaster burn the toast every single time unless I watch it like a hawk????* You know what I would love? To have Consumer Reports do a report on toaster ovens and include mine in their research. I'd bet it would come out so bad that it wouldn't even be placed on their ratings chart, but would have a special paragraph dedicated to it which would be titled "A Worst Buy".

My recommendation to those making Aliyah? Buy your toaster when you get here.

Journal Entry #88: Thursday, December 26

Comparative Narrative

This week two of our close friends were blessed with new babies. One family is native Israeli, while the other just made Aliyah and had their first "sabra". The boy is the seventh generation Israeli, while the girl has the proud title of being the first. Each is the fourth child in the family. The babies, however, are not what I'm comparing.

Sha'arei Tzedek's Maternity Ward

Whoa!! Culture shock!! As a four-time mom and postpartum nurse, I was in for a big surprise on my first visit to an OB unit in an Israeli hospital. Particularly since the woman I visited was my patient in Florida when she had her previous baby. First of all, this is not just an "Israeli hospital". Sha'arei Tzedek is the only Jewish hospital in Jerusalem that is run according to Orthodox, Torah practices. This means that kosher people do not have to eat airplane food. This means that the religious staff rotates who works on Shabbat (after all, it's Shabbat for everyone!) and have lifts arranged for them so that they don't have to drive on Shabbat. This means that you can find phrases from the Torah on plaques on the walls. This means that expectant fathers have a library full of holy books to ponder over when there is time to spend.

Aside from all that, the hospital is in the heart of Jerusalem. If you're lucky enough to have the window bed (as our friend had) you can sit and bond with your brand new baby as you take in the breathtaking view of Jerusalem from the ninth floor of a building that is already situated on a mountain. Can anything be more beautiful??

Nothing's Perfect

The differences have more to do with the pampering that inevitably gets left behind in America's spoiled maternity wards (particularly Boca Raton, where I moved from!) The rooms here are quite small and you're likely to share with one or even two roommates. The meals go to a mother's dining area, though I'm told that if you don't go to your meal, it will come to you. Likewise with pain medications. You need to go ask the nurse for it yourself. And when you do, she's likely to give you nothing more than plain Tylenol.

Visiting hours are also particularly strict. As compared to the guidelines I am accustomed to, of practically an open-door policy with dads allowed 24/7, here even the *fathers* have restricted hours. Lucky us, we came during a no visitors/no fathers hour. A dour-faced security guard sat at the door making sure no illegal visitors wandered in. We sent a message to the room and the dad somehow got the security guard to let us in "for only a minute". One hour later we tiptoed out, and breathed a sigh of relief that the guard had apparently stepped away for a moment. The dad stayed in the room for even though he was extremely thirsty, he was afraid that if he went out for even a minute, he wouldn't be allowed back in. Amazed at our luck at having gotten out unnoticed, we decided to take a chance and buy the poor guy a soda. But, alas, the guard was back in his spot and as dour-faced as ever. I innocently asked him if it was possible to "send" this soda to room #18. He told me to quickly deliver it and come *right back out!* Yes sir! I nearly saluted. I dashed in and made my delivery to a very surprised and grateful dad.

Hadassah – Mount Scopus Maternity Ward

A totally different hospital indeed. Being more on the outskirts of town, it did not have that "city" feel to it. Nor did they feel the need to awkwardly convert their sidewalks into parking lots as the other hospital had! It is a nice, modern building; it has a great, but very different view. It also has a very large number of what was not quite as obvious in Shaarei Tzedek: Arabs. Being as it is in East Jerusalem, it is probably the hospital of choice for residents of that area, most of whom are Arabs. However, it is still an

Israeli hospital with kosher food, just not quite the same religious flavor as the other.

Watch Out For Those Guards!

This guard was posted before we even got to the elevators. She mumbled something in rapid Hebrew that my level-6-Ulpan-Hebrew could barely distinguish but had something to do with getting a pass. She pointed us towards an information booth whose smiling attendant said we could certainly go visit our friend, but didn't give us any sort of pass. Back to the guard we went. She asked us for our pass and we told her the woman said we could go up. So the guard let us up and that was it.

Follow The Schedule That They Don't Give You

We noticed that in this hospital the nurses actually do bring medications to the room. There is still the same new-mother-dining-area, but you can bring the food to your room. That is, if you get there in time before the food is taken away. How do you know when the times are? Well, of course, you have to follow the hospital's schedule. The big question it seems is where in the world does one find the schedule? It is a big question that our poor friend has not yet figured out. Perhaps by the time she is discharged on Sunday she will know how things work there. As for mealtime, I suppose one has to keep their sense of smell on the alert and run to the dining area when you get a whiff of toast.

Shared Practices Between The Two

I know this is going to sound extremely primitive, but (gasp!) there are no TV's in the rooms. But wait – that's not all. There are no telephones in the rooms either. Which brings me to an extremely bizarre (to all of you who have been in American hospitals) practice. The patients all use their cell phones!! I suppose the feeling here is that the cell phone is such a ubiquitous object here that why inconvenience the hospital by placing multiple phone lines in each room, and the patients by making them use expensive phones to which no one knows the number? I've got another question: What about all those warning signs and cell-phone police in the American hospitals that make you feel that you are committing a crime just for using a cell phone? Aren't cell phones supposed to reprogram pacemakers, recalibrate oxygen, and render all defibrillating machines ineffective? Perhaps the holy air in Jerusalem cancels all the ill-effects of cell phone usage in Israeli hospitals. Hmmmm.

Another thing the hospitals have in common is that neither supply their infants with hats. You know, to keep them from losing all their body heat through their head? Oh, and one more thing. Being that these two Jewish babies were born at what is a very festive time of the year outside of Israel, both sets of new parents could appreciate not having their infants photographed wearing a Santa hat. Then again, a Santa hat might be better than no hat at all!!

Journal Entry #89: Sunday, December 29

We're In The Clear

Weather-wise that is. For all those of you who have been imagining our foggy, rainy, freezing winter, the last few days have been absolutely beautiful; still sweater weather, but sunny and clear and not that cold. I'm told that this is more usual for this time of year than what we'd been getting until now. Hey, we're novices! We can only report what we see...

I Feel Like I'm In High School Again

This morning in Ulpan I noticed my classmates studying from some paper I'd never gotten. Feeling all nervous I found out that we were having a TEST that I didn't know about on this paper that I'd never gotten. Knowing from years of experience that "I didn't know" and "I didn't get the review sheet" don't fly as excuses, I just shut up and accepted my fate. Until the test was handed out that is. One look and I knew I was done for. Don't they believe in multiple choice in this country? How am I supposed to fill in the blanks if they don't give me choices? I did not know even one answer. I decided to keep my blank test to myself. Maybe when the teacher would grade the tests she would just assume I'd been absent? I mean, how could I hand in a BLANK TEST??? After the test I sat until break feeling all guilty and thinking of nothing else. In the end I confessed, gave her my blank test, and apologized. She didn't even call my mother or give me detention. In fact I don't even have to take the test tomorrow. Or ever. I think Ulpan is better than high school...

They Don't Do Drills Like These In America

Everyone knows about fire drills. In Florida there are also hurricane drills. I imagine that California has earthquake drills. Maybe Kansas has tornado drills? Well, when my kids started school I must say I was a bit startled to find out they had terrorist drills. Unfortunately necessary. But tonight's drill took the cake. We were with several other new olim (immigrants) at a home in the next town, having our regular support meeting and discussing things like the impending war with Iraq, gas masks, and how to recognize the emergency sirens and what to do if we hear them. Suddenly, as if on cue, we heard an unmistakable emergency siren. What the heck is that all about, we all wanted to know. After unsuccessfully trying to decipher the loudspeaker that we heard from outside, a neighbor was phoned who clued us in: There is an emergency drill outside and not to be alarmed if we hear shooting, because we will, and it is all part of the drill. Oh, and by the way, she added, we must all remain indoors because the shooting will be with live ammunition.

"Is this normal?" we asked of the group moderator who'd been here for forty years. "Actually, I've never known it to happen before," was his reply.

Luckily there was plenty of chocolate cake and popcorn. So we sat and ate and talked until the all-clear was announced. I can think of far worse ways to spend a Sunday evening!

Journal Entry #90: Tuesday, December 31

Tunnel Vision

Today we were treated to a tour of the Western Wall tunnels by our friends who are in from Florida. It was a real treat. The tour guide is renowned for her gruff exterior, impatience for lateness, and her ability to pour her soul into every tour she gives. Ours was no exception. Deep under the Moslem Quarter, at the most holy spot on the Western Wall, she didn't just stand back to allow her tour group to pray. She prayed – and cried – right there with us. Somehow you just knew that she did the same every time she came through the tunnel.

Our Grand Exit

When you're finished with the underground tour you have the choice of exiting all the way back the way you came, or just above you into the Moslem quarter. Our guide gives this option to each group she takes. We hesitantly, though determinedly, chose to exit through the Moslem quarter. You know, there is something very sad about the fact that we are a free people living in our own land and yet most of us are afraid to go to many parts of that land. I can assure you that despite everything, there is no Arab that is afraid to go into ANY part of Israel. This is eminently evident by the huge numbers of Arabs who work in every type of Israeli environment, yet Jews are afraid to even travel on roads that pass close to Arab villages, let alone go into them. Look, I'm not passing judgment; I'm just saying it like it is. Be that as it may, the whole lot of us on the tunnel tours were of the "don't go into the Arab quarter" persuasion. Yet we chose to go anyway. We seemed to have the mutual feeling that we will refuse to inconvenience ourselves out of fear or anything else. So we marched right into the Moslem quarter and proudly (if a little bit huddled together and with a guard on either end) walked all the way back to the Jewish Quarter. Hey, I didn't say we shouldn't take precautions!

Journal Entry #91: Thursday, January 2

Sometimes You Just Have To Go With The Rhythm

Our small house has just become significantly smaller. Somehow the addition of a junior drum set to our house seemed to reduce its size. Why is it that drum sets don't come with a volume control button? Seriously though, Eitan received a drum set for his birthday, last May. We told him we would open it in Israel. Of course we got to Israel, and had to first wait for the lift. Then we got the lift and had to wait until we unpacked. Then we unpacked and had to wait until we unpacked some more. This continued for nearly five months until we finally cleared a space just big enough. And now, alas, we have very loud drums in our house. We will start Eitan on lessons immediately. The goal of the lessons will be for him to learn how to play the drums beautifully without making a sound.

Scary Story Debunked

Remember that live-ammunition drill we had to stay indoors for? Well, it wasn't live ammo. Hey, I can only report what I am told and that's what I had been told. But it made for a dramatic journal!

Journal Entry #92: Saturday, January 11

Miracles Do Happen

...and today was nothing short of one. Ezra actually played, of his own volition, with a Hebrew-speaking boy! I asked him, afterwards, if the boy is his friend. He answered me as only a 6-year-old can: he is not my *speaking* friend, he is just my *playing* friend. Still, I'll take whatever I can get!

Navigating A Strange System

The medical system, that is.

Due to my pregnancy, I hastily chose a physician a few months ago without too much effort. You see, here, unless you get a private doctor, you only see the dude a few times in the whole pregnancy and then a hospital midwife delivers you anyway. That is, if all is well and good, and why shouldn't it be? It should be. But it isn't always. This week I discovered just how important it is to have a good doctor.

A routine test I had gave a not-so-routine result. Though I have been reassured that it is more than likely to be completely fine, I need to thoroughly explore the "less than likely" side to be sure. So picture this: I went to my doctor with this information. He gave me a list of tests to have done, including some I have no idea how to make happen, and then he told ME to call HIM with the results!! Oh, and not to call him until I have ALL of the results. Can you imagine?! I was shocked.

Right away I got on the phone to friends and found out that this does not have to be the case. There are plenty of doctors who actually care, and specialize in what I needed, and I got some unofficial referrals. One of the specialists my doctor told me to go to recommended that I go to one of the doctors I had been "referred" to. She wrote a letter to my doctor making that main recommendation, and I was quite relieved as I set off to deliver the letter and get the referral I so badly wanted. Do you know what? My doctor refused!!

Since crying wasn't helping much, I had my husband call. I'm not exactly sure that the doctor understood that my husband was asking for me to be referred to a different doctor *for good,* and not just for a test or a consult, but at the end of the conversation, he finally said that if I was just too anxious, we could have the secretary write up the referral and tell her that he will sign it. Now I just hope he doesn't look too closely at the referral that we will happily draft for him, because I am NEVER going back to him.

Journal Entry #93: Wednesday, January 15

We Interrupt These Difficulties
To Deal With A Technical Part Of The Program

Technically ridiculous, that is. Remember back in September when our brand-new, and unmanned car was in an accident with an unmanned truck? (Seriously, you just can't make this stuff up!) Of course the unmanned truck was at fault since IT rolled down the hill and into OUR car.

After $10,000 in repairs, we had no choice but to put it all on our credit card as we waited for payment. OBVIOUSLY the payment would come since the fault was a no-brainer and we have all of the photographs, witnesses and police reports to prove it. Right? Wrong. The insurance for the truck company took four months to come up with a way out. And I believe they may be successful. You see, the guy who WASN'T driving the truck wasn't insured to drive it (or stand next to it and watch it roll down the hill either, apparently.)

How did I know that it wasn't going to be as simple as it seemed? Now we will have the pleasure of suing an Arab truck company for money they will undoubtedly claim not to have. Who would have thought we'd have had the opportunity to "learn" so many Israeli bureaucratic systems in our first year of Aliyah? At least our car is working!

And Now, Back To The Difficulties

Persistence pays off. After all the phone calls and tears, I received the medical referral I so badly wanted. So far everything looks okay. As for my doctor, I've decided it's worth it to switch to a private one (i.e. NOT through insurance). It's extremely easy to switch to a private doctor here, since you keep your whole file with you anyway. (No awkward phone calls requesting your records be forwarded). Right now, my peace of mind is worth any price.

Two Weeks To Go And Counting...

After four and a half months, I am ready for Ulpan to be finished. My husband is even more ready than I am, and has decided to quit, cold turkey. (Easiest habit he ever broke.) I, however, am determined to see it through to the end, even if I don't really do the homework, and even though I do so poorly on the tests that I hide mine when its time to hand them in. (Don't tell my kids!) Seriously, though, Ulpan has been incredible and I have not only learned a tremendous amount, but it has been a great social avenue as well. But, well, you know. I guess the "home stretch" of anything always seems the longest. I am kind of wondering when I will be able to really speak Hebrew, though. Maybe it will be the day they hand me that Ulpan certificate?

Journal Entry #94: January 16 – Six Month Review

Language

Despite how I make fun of myself, the reality is that I can now actually have a reasonable conversation in Hebrew, even over the phone. Even better, when I go into a store and talk to the sales help in Hebrew, they no longer feel bad for me and offer to speak to me in English. These are major accomplishments! I can now struggle my way through our neighborhood's weekly newsletter. When we get mail I at least know what the subject matter is even if I don't understand it all.

As for the rest of the family, everyone's Hebrew has improved from where they started. (For some, that means a little more than nothing. But even that is something!) Lawrence knows much more than he lets on, but is quite pleased that in his line of work, Hebrew isn't such a big deal. Which brings us to…

Employment

No, neither of us have jobs. Not yet, anyway. I, however, have not been looking at all. Lawrence has been looking and his efforts seem to be paying off! He has had several very promising interviews and we are hoping that he will soon be employed. If it works out, the timing will have been fantastic since Ulpan is only now finishing for us, so he was able to maximize his Hebrew learning time. All of the possibilities are no further than Jerusalem, so the commute would be a snap.

Food

I know it sounds like a silly topic, but it is something we are involved in at least three times a day (and often much more than that!), so I thought it was worth mentioning. It is also something that involves quite a bit of adjusting and reworking things like shopping lists, menus, and even cooking habits. (Especially when you have a tiny oven!) I can tell you that no one in this house is starving. We have found all of the grocery stores and take-out places within a 35km radius. We know where to get the best bagels, and the tastiest chopped liver. We know where to go if we want the checkout people to help us bag our groceries (and how to get them to do it!) We know where to get the nicest produce, the freshest bread, and the cheapest prices. We learned how to recognize items that look totally different here such as cream cheese, celery, and farina. (Though we haven't yet figured out bleach).

Six months ago we had to be brought to the grocery store and walked through, aisle by aisle, to figure out what in the world we were buying. Now, I think I can honestly say, we can grocery shop completely independently, and even prepare the food that we buy!

The Kids

My four children all came here with very different attitudes. They all had to cope with leaving behind schools, friends, and all things familiar. As children, while their opinions matter, ultimately the decision to make Aliyah was made for them. This imposed upon them a whole different element to their acclimation: The element of living with an enormous change that was someone else's choice.

Life in Israel for them ranged from incredible to miserable depending on everything from the weather, their friends, the food, their bedrooms, and everything else. Over the past six months we have watched incredible transformations in our kids. We now hear our kids asking about where we will permanently settle (Neve Daniel seems the unanimous choice for our children!) We've seen resistance to Hebrew begin to melt away. And unlike us, when our kids speak Hebrew it is with an Israeli accent! Most of our kids have developed strong groups of friends. We've watched the awkwardness and strange feelings of being in a new location be replaced by familiarity and a true sense of belonging.

In Summary

While we still have a long way to go, I can't believe how far we've come. In six short months, our lives have changed in a most unbelievable way. We have left a world of leased luxury cars, and come to a land of long-term owning of multi-passenger, functional vehicles. We left the beautiful manicured grass that is only for show, to a country that puts a playground on every corner. We left tuition-based family size, and arrived to all the choices we could have wanted in schools – and for next to nothing. We've traded in Disney World for the Western Wall.

Are there things we miss? Of course. I still shop at The Gap online. When my family comes, they'll bring us Domino brown sugar, and Quaker oatmeal. And life here isn't perfect. I'll be the first to admit that. But overall? We made the best move we ever could.

Journal Entry #95: Monday, January 20

It's Just Not The Same In America

This past weekend we celebrated *Tu B'Shevat*, the New Year for the Trees. While I have participated in random occasions marking this special day, somehow, a celebration for the trees and special fruits of Israel is just impossible to really appreciate in Boca Raton, Florida. Oh, we would try. Plant seeds, eat carob and dates. Talk about the holiday, sing a song or two. But here, it was totally different. Here it was REAL! What did we do to mark the holiday for the trees in Israel? We planted trees in Israel!! I don't mean that we wrote a check to JNF (an honorable thing to do, no doubt) which is famous for having populated Israel with beautiful forests. I mean that we went to a new area, with many of our neighbors, took picks and shovels, and physically planted trees. Our children loved it. They helped select the site, dig the moist earth, place the teeny sapling just so, carefully fill the little hole, and make a little rock border to protect "our" tree. And all this while overlooking a breathtaking view of the Judean hills. Now THIS is Tu BeShevat!!

No Way Out, No Way In

Last night we stopped by the Dan Pearl Hotel to visit our friends, the Bennetts, who are here visiting. We parked in the hotel's underground lot. When we got to the attendant he asked us how long we'd be there. We told him it would be "under an hour". He then charged us 12 shekel, we paid, and we parked. Two hours later, when we finally left, we wondered how we could get past the guard without him charging us for the extra hour. We went down to the lot, got into our car, and started driving nonchalantly past the guard booth. Funny, but there was no one there. In fact, it actually seemed like the guy had closed up shop. This made no sense, but oh well. At least we didn't have to pay. Our victory was short-lived. You know why the guy wanted to know how long we would be there? The 12 shekels would have been the charge regardless. He asked us because he was going to be locking the whole, darn parking lot!! Nice of him to neglect to mention that to us.

We drove up to the exit, and found that we were on the inside of a sealed-tight garage. We sat for a moment, staring at the locked gate, wondering what in the world to do. I got out of the car to look for any signs of life – anyone who would know how to open the garage. I found a button. I pressed it and I still don't know if it worked a mechanism, or notified someone else who worked a mechanism, but within two minutes the garage was miraculously opening up and we made our quick getaway.

That was the "No Way Out" part of the story. Of course there is more to it. You see, we have a guard booth at Neve Daniel as well. Our guard booth also closes at night. 12:15 a.m. to be exact. We got there at 1 a.m. No problem, you see, everyone in Neve Daniel is issued a key to the gate for those late nights that inevitably occur. Too bad we couldn't find the darn thing. We arrived at the Neve Daniel gate a few moments after we realized that the key was nowhere in sight. We sat at the sealed gate, stuck, only blocks away from our toasty house, and we couldn't get even a foot closer. Hmmm, why did this feel so familiar? Luckily Lawrence has done guard duty at the booth and he found a way in and was able to press the button this time.

Journal Entry #96: Thursday, January 23, 2003

A Tough Conversion

Or, I should say, a "*Taph*" conversion. And one that I can't be bothered with. In my Ulpan class the other day, my teacher looked over my shoulder at my writing and discovered a dreadful problem. Apparently I have been writing my *taphs* (the last letter of the Hebrew Aleph-Bet) incorrectly. She crossed mine out and showed me the proper way to write them.

I looked at her incredulously and all I could say was, "After thirty years you want me to correct my *taph???*"

Who Said Medical Bureaucracy Is Bad In Israel?

Oh yeah, it was me. Well it's not ALL bad. First – I have found a wonderful doctor who is kind, caring, and knowledgeable, gives me time, answers questions, and even gave me his home phone number. I guess my last one was just a dud, and here I was thinking the whole medical system was to blame for one doctor's insufficiencies. What do I know? I'm just a new immigrant.

Wonderful doctor #2 is my children's pediatrician. When he referred one of my children to someone whose earliest available appointment was one YEAR from now, he made a few phone calls, pulled a few strings, and somehow got an appointment for two DAYS later. Talk about service!

A Special First For Us

Today we went to our first Bar Mitzvah at the *Kotel* (Western Wall). It was for the son of our dear friends from Boca Raton, Jody and Rich Bennett. I've been to the Kotel many times, but as a woman I am always at the Wall by myself, as opposed to my husband who will join any ongoing prayer service on the men's side. Today was different. As part of a group, we all congregated next to each other right at the Wall, on either side of the *mechitza* (separation) and had a service together. I can't tell you what it was like, being a part of that. It was so special. And of course, being so close to the family of the bar mitzvah boy only heightened the feelings for all of us.

We plan on spending Shabbat in Jerusalem with them, another first, at least for my children. And something they are all quite excited about, I might add. And what else could I possibly ask for? I have four wonderful children who consider it a most exciting event to spend Shabbat in Jerusalem! This is happiness.

Journal Entry #97: Sunday, January 26

The Honeymoon May Be Over, But The Feelings Are Still There

I'm referring to the "honeymoon" of making Aliyah, of course. I drove my daughter to a Bat Mitzvah today in The Jerusalem Forest. I had never been there before, and the drive through there was immensely enjoyable (once I was assured that the very narrow road I was traveling on was indeed only one-way). But the drive back was even more special. The timing had me driving out of the park near sunset. As I drove through the hills and mountains of Jerusalem, watching the setting sun turn the sky an array of beautiful colors, a most appropriate song started playing on my cassette player, joyfully intoning in Hebrew about the "hills surrounding Jerusalem, now and forever." I guess you could call it a multi-sensory experience. I just called it "Incredible."

Donkey Business

And believe me, I am not making light of it. For those of you who haven't heard, the latest suicide bomber was the four-legged kind. Though I suppose it wasn't the donkey's fault, so you can hardly call it a "suicide". And yes, it was on that Tunnel Road that leads from Gush Etzion to Jerusalem. Many of my friends were in the vicinity right around that time. Apparently the donkey was sent off on its own little death march with a bomb hidden in its pack. Suspicious motorists (though I'm not sure what the donkey did to arouse their suspicion) called the army hotline, but before anything could be done the bomb had exploded. Thank G-d, no one was hurt though some people were treated for shock. Of course the donkey isn't in very good shape. People were momentarily astonished that the Arabs would actually send an innocent donkey to its death, and then they remembered that they shouldn't be surprised. After all, if one sends his own son, why not his donkey?

Our Big News

Lawrence has accepted a job! We are very excited about it. It is in Jerusalem with some really weird hours (5 p.m. – 1 a.m.). That's because it is an American company that is more or less working during American business hours. (NOT American salaries – too bad!) Anyway, the timing is great since we're just finishing Ulpan. (Actually, Lawrence quit Ulpan a few weeks ago, if you remember). I don't know when he is starting, or really much else about it, but we are just thrilled.

Journal Entry #98: Wednesday, January 29

I'll Take A Primitive Voting Process Over Chads Any Day

Yesterday was a momentous occasion for me and my fellow new Israeli immigrants. It was my first opportunity to cast my vote towards the formation of the Israeli Knesset. The 16th Knesset, to be exact. With political campaign signs plastered everywhere, and a decision that was none too easy with people arriving still undecided, I made my way to the Neve Daniel voting booth. I suppose you must call it a booth, for what else would it be? However, it was actually one of those big tri-fold cardboard things that you buy for your fifth grader to do his/her science project on. But yesterday, it was a booth.

So this is the whole complicated procedure: After showing my identification and being approved as an eligible-to-vote-Israeli-citizen, I was handed a little envelope and sent behind the "booth". There, on a table, were twenty-some-odd neat little piles of papers, each with the name and symbol of a different political party. My job was to select the paper of my chosen party, place it in the envelope, and drop the envelope in the ballot box. That's it. As I walked away, clearly surprised at the ease of voting in this country, someone remarked, almost apologetically, that the system here is somewhat primitive.

Primitive? I responded, Who cares, at long as it works! Last time I voted, in the 2000 Presidential election in Palm Beach County, FL, my vote, along with several hundred thousand others, was the laughing stock of the world. What with misread ballots, miscast votes and hanging chads. Now THAT was primitive!

Countdown Until Tomorrow

A most momentous day! A day I have been waiting for for five months! Yes! It is the last day of my Ulpan! I am so happy I took the Ulpan Hebrew course because I really learned a lot. And I am so happy it is over! The funny thing is that they have decided to extend the course one month for a very small fee. I didn't consider it for half a second. The majority of the time I actually enjoyed it and more or less looked forward to it. Okay, maybe that's not entirely true. But in level six there is a lot of homework and tests twice a week! Half the time I wouldn't even know about the test until the teacher was handing it out and then I would panic. Tomorrow is a test that I DO know about, as it is the test you take on completion of the Ulpan, and upon passing you qualify for a certificate that entitles you to speak Hebrew to anyone you like.

Journal Entry #99: Thursday, January 30

"No More Pencils, No More Books..."

Remember how we used to sing that on the last day of school? Well that little sing-song has been joyfully going through my mind all day. ESPECIALLY after that final exam!! First of all, I was completely clueless about the whole format of the test. I seemed to have been the only person in my whole huge Ulpan who didn't realize that the test was being given somewhere else! After Ulpan today we had to get to the center of town, park (a whole event in and of itself), and then assemble in a strange classroom and wait until cows started flying before they finally came to administer the test. As if that wait wasn't bad enough, we had to wait until everyone finished part one before we could start taking part two. I happen to be an extremely fast test taker and I finished around an hour before the last person. It was a very long day. Luckily the test is behind me, the Ulpan is behind me, and I can now sit home all day, every day, and eat bon-bons.

Journal Entry #100: Saturday, February 1

Shocking News

People are in a state of shock. I am in a state of shock. I received the horrible news about the space shuttle Columbia from a neighbor as I was spending the last half hour of a visit with our friends from Boca Raton. They were, as I had been, in Florida back in '86 when the Challenger exploded and today's horrifying news brought back all of those memories.

Colonel Ilan Ramon, one of the astronauts who so tragically lost his life today, was a real hero to the people of Israel, and there is a personal connection right here in Gush Etzion where we live. Yesterday I was in my daughters' school and I was admiring a whole bulletin board display with all of the headlines about Ramon being the first Israeli to go into space and about the shuttle lift-off, and all. It is a really big deal here. In addition to all of that, was a handwritten sign explaining how he is the cousin (or uncle, I'm not sure) to two of the girls in the school. Even without that family relationship, people really felt a connection to him. Everything from his marking Shabbos in space to bringing kosher food on board, all made Jews everywhere, but particularly in Israel, feel a sense of closeness to him.

Similar to Christa McAuliffe, who died aboard the Challenger, perhaps Ramon was simply someone who was made into a real person because of all the hype and many human interest articles about him. He wasn't just a name on a list. He was real. I feel great pain at the loss of all of the astronauts, for their families and for all of America. For Colonel Ramon I feel an additional, almost personal loss because it feels as if we knew him.

Having lived for the past nine years in Florida, we also felt a strong connection to the space shuttle having watched numerous lift-offs from our own back yard. (We may have been a three-hour drive from Cape Canaveral, but once the shuttle was in the air it could be seen for miles around). I suppose that being a Jew, an Israeli, and an American all contributes to and compounds the sense of loss in this particularly tragic event.

5

Preparing...

Journal Entry #101: Monday, February 3

Aliyah: Phase II

Wow, life is suddenly very different. I don't miss Ulpan one bit. In fact, though I won't know if I passed the Ulpan exam for a few weeks, (and I don't think I aced it so it's a bit iffy), I was in a store today and the shopkeeper thought my Hebrew was very good for having been here seven months. That's good enough for me! Even if they couldn't understand the word I used for "purple" which apparently hasn't been used since the time of the Bible.

My husband's work, however weird the hours are, seems to be great. He likes the company very much and enjoys the people he works with. It's also very nice to be among the vast majority as an Orthodox Jew at work, instead of one of the only ones. Not only does he not have to explain about keeping kosher, but there are TWO kosher microwaves at work: Meat and Dairy. Not only does he not have to duck out periodically for daily prayers, but there is a substantial *minyan* (quorum of men) for each prayer service. Jewish holidays? There's no question – he's off for all of them.

How about us at home? After all, we've become accustomed to family dinnertime for the past seven months. So far, the kids have been setting his place as if he were merely going to be home "a little late". I leave it there for him so he knows he was missed. But we are taking advantage of the situation in that we can have French toast or pancakes for dinner. And we don't need to serve a green vegetable. (Strawberries were our veggies tonight! Who says vegetables have to be green??) Life will be a little different. But, as I've always said, different doesn't have to be a bad thing – and usually isn't.

Clean The House: Company's Coming!

Though I'm sure she won't care what the house looks like. After all, it's my mom who's arriving! And what perfect timing. Right after I've finished Ulpan, and my husband started working. For the next ten days I can spend my time in the malls and shops with my own mother. (What? You thought she was coming to tour??)

Journal Entry #102: Wednesday, February 5

Hebrew? What Hebrew?

Last night I had the very joyful task of picking up my mom from Ben-Gurion Airport. As I was waved through the airport entry checkpoint by a soldier, I was pulled over by a cop. Stunned by the simultaneous event, I pulled over next to the cop, wondering what I could have possibly done wrong. As the police officer approached me, I found that I could not remember a single word of Hebrew. Not the word for "excuse me" or "what happened" or even "hello" or "goodbye". In fact, it was somewhat embarrassing to pull out my Israeli driver's license (I was tempted to only show my American one!) and not be able to say even a word in Hebrew. It turns out that I had done nothing wrong; it was simply a random check.

I still don't know how I did on my Ulpan test, but I certainly flunked the Hebrew "stress test"!!

A Taste Of My Experience

One of the things I have been appreciating so much is every little experience as a citizen, instead of as a tourist. Like not having a camera with me 24/7. Or like voting in the Israeli elections. Or just the fact that we don't have to see everything, or even anything, in a hurry, because we are here to stay and can see things when we want to.

Enjoying Bubbie's visit

My mother is having a unique experience as well. Having been here many times, including once a year for the past four years, she has been to many places all over the country. However, this visit is different. As she has said to me, she, too, feels different now. Though she is not a citizen of Israel, she no longer feels quite like a tourist. She is simply a mom visiting her daughter. And to prove that fact, we did just what we said we would do: We went shopping! We spent her first day here at the Jerusalem Mall (Malcha), just a mother and daughter together. Then, just to make sure she felt like a native, we took every type of local transportation to get home. Of course, it would have had a more authentic feel if we knew what we were doing while we were doing it!

For example, we took a city bus towards the Gush Etzion bus stop. But we didn't know where the closest stop was to where we were going, so we missed it! The nice bus driver realized what had happened, so he let us off and directed us several blocks to our destination. When we were still too far to catch the bus, we saw it approaching the bus-stop. Not wanting to wait another hour for another bus, we decided to run for it anyway. Of course we missed it, but I'm sure we entertained the passing cars as the two of us ran futilely down the busy street. Our efforts did pay off, however, since we caught a bus right after we got there. Not the right bus, but at least it would leave us off at the bottom of the (very big) Neve Daniel hill.

This gave us the opportunity to hike up the mountain, and, shortly after beginning our trek, to hitchhike to the top. Okay, so maybe we did not utilize EVERY form of local transportation, but we did manage more than if I'd simply DRIVEN to the mall!! (Which I wish I would have done!)

Journal Entry #103: Sunday, February 9

Our Sink Has Sunk

Literally. It all started way back in August when our landlord finally vacated the downstairs portion of the house. After a toilet seat was installed, among other minor things, the downstairs bathroom was finally usable. Then one day we noticed that items in the under-sink cabinet were wet. On careful examination we discovered that the sink was not firmly attached to the countertop, causing a little leak. Knowing our landlady to be in no hurry to get things fixed, we decided to get an estimate for her. She thought the estimate, which included securing the sink with a brace, was ridiculously high, and said that she would come and fix it herself with silicone (her favorite fixing tool). She never came.

Over the weeks, the sink slowly, slowly separated ever so slightly more from the countertop. We heard through the grapevine that our landlady believed us at fault, that perhaps we had stood in the sink and started jumping in it. Right. So I called her right away to explain that we had never

Just don't turn on the water

jumped in the sink (I didn't need to keep a straight face since it was over the phone), yet the sink was truly separating from the counter and it had better be fixed or eventually it would come off completely. Of course nothing happened.

At this point my husband had had it and decided to just make the appointment with the guy to fix it and take the cost off of the rent. The plan would have been perfect if only the guy had shown up today as scheduled. Instead he didn't show up, and a few short hours ago when I went to wash my hands in the bathroom, the sink was gone. In the countertop where the sink had been was a perfect oval hole that gives one a clear view of a sideways sink laying atop all of our neatly arranged toiletries.

Right away I called my landlady to tell her about the recent turn of events. I told her I was having the fix-it guy come to fix the sink. She insisted that it was unnecessary and way too expensive and that she was going to come and fix the sink with silicone one day this week. Exasperated, I tried to explain that her stupid silicone was just not going to do the trick and what will we do until she gets here? No matter, Lawrence said he's going to get the fix-it guy anyway. I told him that from now on *he* would be the one to speak with our landlady.

Journal Entry #104: Monday, February 10

Local Sound Effects

We were watching one of the "new" movies on DVD that my mom brought from the states. This one was "Swiss Family Robinson" that Disney made back in 1960. We were enjoying it with our surround-sound system, though I must say that in 1960, movies weren't particularly set up for such a system. However, in one scene, as the Robinson family is preparing for an attack by pirates, a fuse on a bomb is accidentally set off. I was amazed as I watched the little fire wind its way across the fuse as the noise got intensely louder and we could actually feel the fuse snaking its way right on top of us. In fact, I believe the house actually shook. Or perhaps it was only us who were shaking, such was the reaction of so unexpected an effect. It took us a moment until we realized that it was not a sound effect after all, but a low-flying army jet whose pilot was blissfully unaware of the movie enhancement he had contributed to.

Effects Of The Local Sound

In such a small country it is not at all unusual to see and hear army aircraft. After all, if they're going to fly, they don't have too many choices as to where! Now, with all of the Iraq talk and plans and whatever, it does seem that the flights are somewhat more often.

Lexi recently mentioned the impending war with Iraq and wanted to know if we should be afraid. That was a tough question. I told her that America has a powerful army and a well-thought out plan. I told her that Israel has the strongest army in the Middle East and that America will do everything it can to protect her. Most importantly, I told her that G-d is the strongest of all, and that people can plan all they like, but we don't pray to the people, we pray to G-d.

Journal Entry #105: Friday, February 14

The Interesting Life Of An Oleh

Featured in the Sun Sentinel

Actually, at this point our life seems so ordinary that yesterday, when our reporter friends who are here from the Sun Sentinel newspaper in Florida asked us what we'd be doing that might be interesting to photograph, I couldn't think of anything. Luckily the article they're doing now is only incidentally about us, being that they are mostly here to see what will be with the most publicized and most under-fought war in history. It was a lot of fun for our kids who greeted the reporters as old friends. Particularly for Ezra who was walking home from the bus stop with his friends, to find his photographer buddy snapping away as they were coming down the stairs.

Come to think of it, I guess it's not the most ordinary thing in the world to have newspaper reporters from your home town coming to your new home 6,000 miles away to interview you.

Touring With My Mom

Did I say we weren't going to go touring? We toured all over the place! In fact we must have gone to every single shopping mall in Jerusalem. I now know where to buy just about anything you might need in this area. Hey, this was important!! (And lots of fun!)

Living With The Calendar I Live With

I vaguely recall some sort of holiday around now. I don't know. The only thing it says on my calendar is that Shabbos is tonight. I did see some hearts in a few stores. Perhaps that had something to do with it...

Journal Entry #106: Sunday, February 16

Life Is All Perspective

After the Code Orange was issued in the U.S. my friend emailed me about the different preparations they were considering and how it was affecting her. She added: "We were told today...what to do in case of evacuation or bombing. It's really scary. I don't know how you live with this on a daily basis."

I had been reading with a sympathetic ear (eye?) the whole time until the last sentence that referred to me. Wait a minute, I thought, I'm not living with any such thing on a daily basis. I'm simply living. I send my kids to school, my husband goes to work, I shop, do laundry, bake, read, surf the internet, practice Hebrew with telemarketers, you know, regular stuff. I don't carry my gas mask in my purse. I haven't emptied our local grocery store's contents into the little sealed room in my house that happens to be my boys' bedroom. I don't live in a state of paranoia or fear. What struck me was, Why don't I?

I think there are a number of clear differences between threats of the "same" nature to Israel and to the U.S. (At least this is MY perspective.) In Israel, unfortunately, threats have always been part of the reality. People grow up with that, and there are many cultural adaptations to it, particularly military and intelligence, not to mention a certain amount of diligence and preparedness by the ordinary citizen. America, on the other hand, has grown up with a feeling of being somewhat disconnected, continentally, from the ills of war and terror. 9/11 notwithstanding, people still have those feelings of being protected and that has engendered a different sort of attitude among the ordinary citizen and those who are assigned to protect them. (Being everyone from top-military brass down to the $6/hr luggage checker.)

You see, it's not that we live with *fear* on a daily basis. It's that we don't take our safety and security for granted. I suppose that once you're in that frame of mind, it's only a difference between a "regular" security threat vs. a big one. Truthfully, I don't find all the preparations much different than what was recommended in Florida at the start of every summer as we prepared for hurricane season. (And there are plenty of people who don't bother with that either!)

Bottom line is that if one must live with the fear of something, better to be among people who are experienced at handling that sort of thing. Ever been stuck in a snowstorm in Neve Daniel? Believe me, you'd be stuck! They just aren't equipped to handle it. One main road gets plowed, and the rest of the town is simply snowed in. Unfortunately Israel is *very* experienced in war and terror attacks. That may keep some people away. But it can happen anywhere, and when, G-d forbid, it does, the best place to be is where they know how to handle it best.

Journal Entry #107: Sunday, February 23

Sudden Realizations

As we get on with our daily life, I occasionally notice some trivial little thing in a big way. For example, today I brought Eitan to school, late, after a dental appointment. Nothing particularly new and unusual. But as my eight-year-old got out of the car in front of that big, Israeli school, where many hundreds of Hebrew-speaking kids spend their days, I watched as he made his way down the sidewalk, completely at ease. I observed him walk through the gate, share a brief exchange with the security guard, and continue his way quite comfortably into the building. Wow, I thought to myself, it's as if he was always here! At least in that one encapsulated moment...

Another one: When we first made Aliyah, we did it via a 6,000 mile plane trip and felt it for a long time thereafter. In other words, despite being in my homeland, we were still 6,000 miles away from the United States, and from all of the familiar trappings that we had called "home" for the last thirty-some-odd years. As time went on we slowly, slowly began to become accustomed to our new life here. The strange and different started to be familiar and comfortable. The neighborhoods, the roads, the shopping (we all know about that!), the schools, the language, the culture, and all the little idiosyncrasies of life in the most disputed land in the Middle East.

One day, all of a sudden, I had this sudden flash of realization: It isn't strange at all anymore! Despite the many continued challenges that the future (and present) hold for us, I feel just as at-ease as Eitan looked walking into school today. I realized that I feel that I am "home". (Now if only we can get our landlady to renew our rental contract for another year without raising the rent...)

Speaking Of The Landlady...

For all those waiting with bated breath for an update on the sink, unfortunately there is nothing to tell. The landlady wouldn't allow our guy to fix the sink since she felt he was too expensive. Meanwhile, she hasn't gotten anyone else, and the sink has been settling comfortably down below among our spare shampoo bottles and rolls of toilet paper. I had been brushing my teeth in the kids' bathroom, until I discovered that my toothbrush is quite appealing and has been used on more than one occasion, by someone who is not me. Now I use the utility sink.

The Continuing Saga Of Our Car Crash

Now this story is just begging for a happy ending. This would mean only one thing – a big, fat check payable to us to cover all of the money we laid out to fix our car. It hasn't happened yet, but we are ever optimistic...

Journal Entry #108: Monday, February 24

Let It Snow, Let It Snow, Let It Snow...

Okay, now that it has our permission, is it actually going to happen??? Well I can't complain even if we don't get the originally forecasted 36 hours of snow, because we did get some snow! In fact, around here when any accumulated snow falls, people are basically homebound (or work-bound, or bound to wherever you happened to be when the snow starts to fall in earnest.) So any snow is really a whole event.

Ironically, we were unable to provide any of the requisite signs of panic or stocking-up when the Sun Sentinel reporters interviewed us about our preparations for The War. But when those first few flakes started coming down today, I high-tailed it to our local grocery store!

Stocking Up

I had been totally lazing this morning and was somewhat oblivious to the expected weather. Around noon my husband received a call urging him to stay home from work due to the likelihood of getting stuck there. Incredulous, I asked Lawrence if he thought it would really snow today. I turned around and looked out the window to discover that it was already snowing!

Oh, no! I realized that we had no milk, and hardly a good supply of food to get us through any extended period of being snowed-in. I hurriedly dressed, figuring on going to Efrat to do a quick grocery shopping. Six minutes later, I was out in my car that already had an opaque layer on all of the windows. With inch-thick snowflakes mixed with hail and a lot of wind, I decided to do my shopping at the dinky little grocery store at the top of the hill in Neve Daniel. Very local seemed to be the intelligent choice.

Of course at the top of the hill the wind is only worse. I made my way from the car to the *makolet* while the wind whipped stinging hail into my face. Almost as soon as I got in to the makolet, the electricity went out in there. So I groped around in the semi-blackness for things I thought we couldn't live without during a snow-in, like tuna fish, eggs and Snickers bars. I grabbed food like there was no tomorrow. I even bought yeast, in case our bread ran out. Luckily the electricity came on eventually, so I could put the finishing touches on my shopping spree, in the light.

I battled the wind to put the groceries in the car, and at that point knew my kids had all been sent home early. So I figured I'd just wait for them, since the bus stop was there as well. And as long as I was waiting, I thought of just a few more things to get at the makolet. You can never be too prepared!!

My Snow-Deprived Kids

So, I saved them the entire dreadful walk home in that miserable weather, forced them to stay outside the extra few seconds to help me bring groceries in, then finally we could all go inside our toasty, warm house and relax. Right? Wrong! They wanted to go outside and PLAY in that gross stuff. But kids, I tried to explain, this is not the kind of snow you play in. It's wet, and slushy, it makes hard, painful snowballs, and you'll get all wet. Besides, we're expecting lots more. Why don't you wait until we get the good stuff?

Of course my pleas fell on deaf ears. Or, should I say, too-many-years-spent-in-Florida-without-snow ears. Out they went, and wet they got. But I suppose it was nothing that a steaming mug of hot chocolate couldn't cure, and thanks to the stash my mother brought me, just in time, I was able to "cure" them all.

But What About Now?

It seems that Israel has not yet been conquered by the science of meteorology. The continuous snowfall that was supposed to commence this evening and not end until Wednesday morning isn't exactly following instructions. After all the urgings of our friends, for Lawrence to stay home from work tonight, he saw no snow for a while and went. I've been sitting home watching for it to get bad so I could call him and tell him he MUST come home this minute. But it isn't bad. I guess he has to stay at work.

Journal Entry #109: Tuesday, February 25

A Very WHITE Day

Yessss! We got our snow! In fact, despite Accuweather.com's continued forecast of "rain" for this area, we still got SNOW! And we are very happy about it. At 6:45 a.m. the kids woke me to take them outside, to play in the fresh surprise that the sky provided for us. I somehow managed to convince them that we should wait until 10 a.m., silently praying that the snow wouldn't turn to rain, knowing I would NEVER be forgiven.

At 10 a.m., true to my word, I bundled up, along with my kids, and we ventured out into a true winter wonderland. Don't ask me how much snow we got. After all, Accuweather says we got nothing. Local media reported 8 inches in Jerusalem, so I imagine we have that or more. (Of course it is now 3:30 p.m. and it has been snowing on and off all day with much more expected!) With half the neighborhood out, we got right into it with snowball fights, snowmen, snow angels and sledding. Not that a sled is a household item in these parts, however the political signs from the recent election seemed to do a great job. We even saw two people SKI down the hill.

Let's build a snowman

Though I'm sure it wasn't fun bringing the skis back UP the hill.

With any luck, tomorrow will be another day like today!

Journal Entry #110: Wednesday, February 26

What a Snowstorm!

We woke up with so much more snow than yesterday, that it was hard to believe. The cars all looked short because the level of the road was so drastically raised. Now I don't know what Accuweather.com would say, but my spatial skills are pretty good and I'd say we got snow in the range of 1 ½ feet! Another day of no school, no work, and lots of outdoor fun. People got even more creative with what they used for sleds and we actually saw a few bathtubs making their way down the hills with delighted occupants. (I kid you not!)

The storm was not without its less desirable effects, such as repeated loss of power through the night resulting in our heat cutting itself off, and Lawrence having to restart it in the middle of the night. Additionally, the whole *yishuv* (neighborhood) lost its phone service, and, along with that, internet service. Oh well, it's just temporary.

Snow-Gear Deficiency

Now that we were truly dumped with snow, we got a chance to put all of our snow gear to the test. Too bad we don't have any. Thanks to a one-time ski trip with our girls, we have a few Gap outfits of fleece pants and sweatshirts. Not exactly waterproof! The girls have boots, the boys have decent gloves, and everyone had a hat. And that was about the extent of it. I made everyone wear three layers of pants to try to keep their legs dry. It didn't work. My poor little Ezra was so wet! His shoes were getting stuck in the very-deep snow, and as he would walk he would step right out of them and I would dig them out.

Nonetheless, we all got plenty of the usual snow-fun in: snowball fights, fort building, sledding, playing, snow-angels, even just walking through it was an adventure!

Journal Entry #111: Monday, March 3

Updates

Phone service: Still without it! I've been calling *Bezeq* (the phone company) daily, and they always say it will be fixed in a few hours. I hang up every time wondering if we're having a language problem...

Kids: Lexi has been back in regular school (no longer in the special Ulpan) for a few weeks now and is very happy. This week we put Shira back in school as well. We're hoping the language will just seep in through osmosis...

Car Insurance: They still have not sent us the very huge check to cover all the money we laid out to fix our car. Maybe there is something in that system we still don't know...

Our Sink: Still sunk. But hopefully the guy will be coming to fix it shortly.

Our Attitudes: Great!! Thank G-d, Lawrence has work, and work that he enjoys at that. The kids are really acclimating, and we're all very happy.

Journal Entry #112: Thursday, March 6

Our Phone Line Is Back!

Here's a great lesson in "it's not WHAT you know, it's WHO you know". Monday, after too many days of calling Bezeq and having no luck, I had a Hebrew speaking friend call to see if she could get any further information. She was told that there were still many people without phone service and they needed to actually come out here to fix the problem, but they couldn't because they didn't "have a bulletproof vehicle available, and wouldn't have one until Thursday." Stunned at the fact that they couldn't find such a vehicle, but more so that they even felt the need for one, she reminded them that 10,000 people drive these roads every day, but to no avail.

Believe me, I wasn't going to take THAT sitting down! Right away I called Shaul Goldstein, the Mayor of Gush Etzion, who seemed even more upset than I was (if that's even possible).

"I will take care of it," he promised me.

Well, what do you know? Tuesday morning at 10:30 a nice man from Bezeq came to my house in a *regular* Bezeq truck, and now my line is fixed! Unfortunately it didn't fix my internet connection because apparently the lightning from the snowstorm (isn't that weird?) fried our computer modem, which seems to have caused the phone-line problem to begin with. But lucky for me, my husband is a computer guy and he plugged some sort of doodad into the computer and now it works.

But That's Not All

Today we received a big, fat check from our car insurance company to cover the damages incurred from the accident back in October! Sometimes all you need is a little faith and a little patience. Okay, maybe A LOT of patience! So what that they wrote the check out to our bank instead of to us? Five minutes in the bank and the check was signed over to us, and deposited in our account!

Journal Entry #113: Monday, March 10

Only In Israel

A friend of ours was riding a bus on a Friday afternoon, when a youth boarded and asked the bus driver to please let him ride without paying, since it was the last bus before Shabbat, and he didn't have any money. The bus driver told him he couldn't. The teen pleaded with him saying that he needed to get home to his family before Shabbat. The bus driver said he could lose his job, and anyway, how could he know that this boy wasn't there expressly to try to get him, the driver, to let him ride for free, resulting in his being fired? (You know, from the teenaged Get-The-Bus-Driver-In-Trouble Association)

At that point many of the passengers who had been observing this interchange started rooting for the boy, asking the bus driver to give him a break and let him ride, which the driver adamantly refused. Finally a passenger on the bus reached into his wallet and announced that he would pay the boy's fare.

"No," announced the driver, standing up and reaching into his own pocket, "I will pay his fare!" And with that he paid the full fare, pulled off a receipt, which he handed to the stunned teen, and continued driving his route.

Classic Or Classical?

Actually, non-classifiable is more like it. In my never-ending quest to find a good radio station, I seemed to have found one worthy of a memory button in our car. Only thing is, I never know what I'm going to hear on it. It seems to play the full gamut of songs from English to Hebrew, 1950s to 2000s, fast to slow. I mean, how in the world do you classify a station that can play uncensored Eminem and then go right into The Carpenters?

Journal Entry #114: Wednesday, March 12

Language Lost

A funny thing happened when I finished my Ulpan. I stopped needing my Hebrew and now I can barely remember anything I've learned! Come on, you know what I mean: Didn't you forget the entire year's worth of

Chemistry right after you took your final exam? I know I did. Except that this time it wasn't supposed to happen that way. But it did. So now I need to find opportunities to maintain what I've learned.

Opportunity #1

Last night my friend and I hosted the monthly gathering for Bat-Mitzvah aged girls in the community, and their mothers. The event is supposed to include some sort of learning and an activity, though I wouldn't really know since I'd never gone before. Anyway, my friend wasn't so thrilled about speaking in public and asked me to do the honors. Of course it was to be entirely in Hebrew but I consented anyway. Suddenly I realized that I might not only make a total fool of myself, but mortally embarrass my daughter in the process. Well, I couldn't let that happen! I jumped right into the task of thoroughly researching what I would present, writing it up as well as I could in my Kindergarten Hebrew, and having my Israeli neighbor jack it up a few notches of intelligence. It was a success! I read it straight from the paper, but so what? Luckily no one asked questions since I had no script of answers prepared. The best part? My daughter was proud of me!

Opportunity #2

Well now that I can teach in Hebrew, surely I can learn in Hebrew as well, right?? Tonight I attended a lecture given by a very popular teacher. The lecture was in Hebrew, but since the teacher is American, I figured I might be able to follow it. I don't know how she was able to talk so fast in Hebrew! (and she *wasn't* reading from a script!) The end of it all is though I did not catch every word, I had a much easier time with her American-accented Hebrew and I certainly understood 2/3 or more. That's good enough for me!

The bottom line is that I took Chemistry because I had no choice. I took Hebrew because I wanted to be able to speak Hebrew. For all those months I was immersed in the Ulpan, I took for granted that all that I was learning would just stay with me for all time. Why, I don't know, since it's never happened that way before. But I've learned a valuable lesson:

If you don't use it, you lose it!

Journal Entry #115: Sunday, March 16

Inspiration From Out Of The Blue

Shira came in the house the other day from taking out the garbage and said something so incredible that I'm not even quite sure what triggered it.

(Certainly not the garbage dumpster!) Maybe it was a combination of being outside in the beautiful, blue-sky weather, with crystal clear views of miles around, then walking in the door to the scents and smells of pre-Shabbat cooking. Who knows? But my 13-year-old said, "It's so amazing! I can't believe we live in Israel!" If you've ever uprooted a teenager from her life, you can appreciate the value of those ten words.

Getting In The Spirit Of Purim

Wow!! There is nothing like Purim in Israel. And it isn't even Purim yet! This special holiday, commemorating the story of the book of Esther, includes dressing up in costume as part of the celebration process. Though the holiday isn't until tomorrow night, all of the schools held their festivities today. Somehow, almost every one of my kids left something at home today so I had an opportunity to visit each school. The costumes were incredible! The kids really pulled out the stops with truly original, creative, and some quite elaborate costumes. Even the teachers and administration got in on the act! One of my favorites in the adult-category was the tough, no-nonsense female security guard who was sporting one of those multi-colored, curly clown wigs.

Purim Costumes

Oh, And About Iraq...

What do you think? This time is it for real? We're about to have a holiday and America is about to go to war? Talk about timing... Most people I've spoken to are not too worried about Scuds this time around. Nonetheless, people have stocked up on food staples and water, and have plastic and tape to seal rooms, if necessary. We keep stocking up on food, and then we keep eating it all. ("Kids, those cookies are for the war!!" I guess we need to buy less tempting war-rations.) Anyway, since the Allies don't exactly have the element of surprise, I hope they have a few other tricks up their sleeve. All we can do now is pray. (As my mother always says, from here it is a local call.)

Journal Entry #116: Wednesday, March 19

Our First Purim

It was amazing, unbelievable and loads of fun! The kids really enjoyed the festivities, as did their parents. Okay, enough about that. Now for the interesting stuff.

We Finally Made It To Hebron

Joining a trip that we happened to find out about, we went on an excursion for *Shushan Purim* (the day after Purim, also the day that Purim is celebrated in Jerusalem and other cities that were walled in ancient times) to the Jewish communities of Hebron, and to *Me'arat Hamachpeilah* (the Cave of the Patriarchs). I'm embarrassed to say that I did not feel 100% safe and comfortable on this trip. Perhaps it was because our guide could think of nothing to point out on the way there other than the sites of recent murders. In view of the fact that he was also our sole armed guard, I was less than thrilled when the bus dropped us off at the Me'arat Hamachpeilah and disappeared. Only then did our guide realize that he had left his Uzi on the bus. Since my husband had gone to work early today, I had no one to assist me in keeping the boys from running to explore every interesting looking thing they saw. Other than that, it was a great trip...

Me'arat Hamachpeilah was very meaningful. Even Ezra was able to relate to the four couples who are buried there. He was especially excited about Adam and Eve with whom he has a fascination, since they were never "born."

Next Stop: Sussiah

Never heard of it? Neither had I. But it is a very cool ancient Jewish city that existed between 300 and 900 C.E. and then abruptly disappeared, though no one knows why. Anyway, we started out by going to this huge underground *mikvah* (ritual bath) which has been transformed into a theater for viewing an audio-visual show about Sussiah. This part was truly a highlight for my boys: They had never seen an ancient movie theater before! (They wanted to know if the movie equipment was ancient too).

The News Bulletin That Burst My Balloon

Okay, okay. I've been telling everyone all along that life is regular and normal and we're just doing our thing and all that has been true. However, tonight it has been announced that we should open and assemble our gas masks and keep them on hand. No matter how normally I'm living my life, it is just not normal to walk around with a gas mask!!

Even Better

I just dug up my favorite Kipling backpack in the school busses' lost-and-found. It was all moldy and gross since my son had left it on the bus months ago. Now let me ask you: In one week's time, how many gas masks do you suppose will be getting moldy in that lost and found? My 6-year-old is going to school with a backpack, a lunch box, and a GAS MASK?? Do you think it's kosher to stow his lunch in the gas mask box? Perhaps I can decorate the outside of the box as a Batman motif lunchbox and pretend the gas mask is an accessory for a new villain called Gasman.

Journal Entry #117: Thursday, March 20

From Purim Masks To Gas Masks

Okay, we did it. Our gas masks have all been assembled thanks to 8-year-old Eitan who paid attention in Gas-mask Assembly Class. Last night I used all of my efforts just to get them down from on top of a very tall closet. (They were kind of "accessible"). Then I opened one box, and decided to deal with it in the morning. Good thinking, because in the morning I had Eitan and he knew just what to do.

I couldn't help but feel a little dorky as I toted my boys off to school, all three of us with our gas masks. Then I arrived at Eitan's school and saw other kids carrying their gas masks. I kind of flipped. It was like, whoa! This is for real. Eitan was basically unaffected, however. He just put it over his shoulder along with his backpack and marched into school.

Then it was time to take Ezra. Concerned about his reaction, I asked him what he thought of the gas mask. He answered: "I have the coolest mask, because mine is like an astronaut." This is quite true, since the rest of ours make us look like we've been transformed with Jeff Goldblum in "The Fly," while Ezra has this whole helmet/vest/waistpack/blower contraption thing that just may end up in the costume drawer one day. He's proud of his!

Not to be deterred from giving my child some badly needed therapy, I asked him how he felt about the need to carry the whole cardboard case around. Apparently, my son has the answer to everything. He thought it could pass as a little suitcase and people might think he's carrying clothes. And that was that. He marched out of the car, said goodbye, and went into school. Still unconvinced, I checked with one of his teachers to be sure that everything was okay, and that I didn't need to know anything additional. She was quite proud of me that I knew to send my son with his mask, and that I had even assembled it as per instructions.

Well, of course, I sent him with a mask, I thought wryly. After all, he's been going with a (Purim) mask all week, why should today be any different?

The Trendy New Accessory

Not wanting to alter my plans, due to such a minor event as a war, I kept my girls home today, as we had been planning for the past week, so that we could go shopping, for dresses for my sister's wedding. (Hey, we have no Sundays off, and Lawrence takes the car right when the kids get home from school. Taking them out of school is the only way!) Anyway, there was something rather fascinating about seeing Israelis of every stripe (including the Arabs) walking through the mall, with their trusty gas masks. In fact, my kids found it almost amusing to see all of the men carrying them about like little purses. We were also quick to notice all those who were not carrying them (definitely the minority) and then we would speculate on whether someone nearby was holding it for them, or if they were just dumb.

The Trendy New Accessory Has Glitches

After opening and assembling all six of our gas masks, we discovered that one of them was missing the little Atropine injection that comes with it. I figured that while I'm at the mall I'll run in to the gas mask booth and get it. After all, everyone should have their masks at this point so it should be a quick little errand. Booth? Who was I kidding? They took over a whole area of the underground parking lot! The line was so long, that I thought I MUST be in the wrong place. But I was wrong. Since EVERYONE opened their gas masks on the same day, and EVERYONE wanted their mask in perfect working order, or else why bother having it at all, EVERYONE who had a problem went to have it fixed immediately. Problems ranged from wrong size, missing piece, broken blowers (on the little-guy "astronaut" suits) to who-knows-what else. After quite a wait, I got the little injector that I hope we'll never need. But I sure would rather have it and not need it, than G-d forbid need it and not have it.

Journal Entry #118: Saturday, March 22

Short-Lived Trend

We went to a town called Chashmonaim for Shabbat to attend the Bar Mitzvah of a close family friend. Of course we had all of our gas masks along with our suitcases and everything else. Figuring that we'd be carrying our gas masks around anywhere we went, we left our suitcases at the homes we were staying at and took the six gas masks along to our host's house.

At a Friday night dessert reception at the synagogue, we left our gas masks at our hosts' home a bit uncertainly, but in good company since all of our Israeli hosts left them there too. (It's only a two minute walk – you have three minutes from the time the alarm sounds to get them on). Anyway, we noticed that of all of the dozens of people there, we saw only one couple with their masks, and a friend of the Bar Mitzvah boy had his as well. Of course the friend was the only American kid (besides ours) in attendance and a brand new immigrant at that. And trust me, you DON'T want to be the only one of many 12-year-olds in attendance with any particular thing that no one else has.

The rest of Shabbos was more of the same. People just weren't carrying them around. Now, mind you, these people would all bring their gas masks to work, or to the mall or wherever, but to simply walk around the neighborhood, they all felt they would have enough time to run back to their homes, if necessary. Not quite understanding the point of having the gas masks if they are not ready to stick on at a moment's notice, I asked some of the veteran Israelis why they weren't carrying them. Apparently, the difference was that they had lived through the previous Gulf war. At that time, the Scuds came flying almost immediately and the gas masks were on and off for weeks. This time, once 48 hours went by and, thank G-d, nothing happened, people just kind of relaxed. We Americans, on the other hand, are addicted to news reports and treat official warnings from the IDF as serious business. Not to mention that our culture tends to make us more careful and conscientious about things. (Maybe "nervous" would be a better word) Hence, the drastic difference in our relationship to gas masks.

Journal Entry #119: Monday, March 24

Memorable Milestone

Last night, we went to a special party at Ezra's school, where the children received their first *chumashim* (Five Books of Moses). I have attended such a party for each of my children, in the past. This one was all the more special, being in Israel. Come to think of it, in retrospect, the accomplishment was exactly equal in the states. I suppose it was just the feeling of my son receiving his first *chumash,* while in the Holy Land. Or perhaps it was simply arriving at this landmark in the year. Actually, it probably had something to do with those adorable Israeli accents that the children recited their lines in. Or, more specifically, that MY son recited his lines in. Yup, I think that was it. It was the accent.

We Went Touring Today

Though you won't find this site in the typical tourist books. We took a tour of the maternity ward in Shaarei Tzedek hospital in Jerusalem. Of course the tour was all in Hebrew. I think I got the general idea, though I'm not sure about my husband. One thing that was very clear to me: the experience will be like none I've had before. Having worked in a maternity ward in Boca Raton, Florida, I have a certain perspective of how things operate in such units. They don't operate that way here! In the hospital I worked at, the women NEVER shared a room, yet they complained about sharing a bathroom. Here I'll be lucky if I only have ONE roommate. I will also have to go to my meals – no room service here. And if I want my baby at night, I will have to go to the baby. BUT – I will have my baby in JERUSALEM! Isn't that awesome?? Give me ten roommates. Who cares?? We would all be having our babies in Jerusalem!

Journal Entry #120: Friday, March 28

The Brighter Side?

I always say to look at the bright side of things. You know, there is a teeny bright side to having a war going on practically in your backyard. It is that now when I check for the weather report on accuweather.com, the weather in the Middle East is actually a headline! Of course it still doesn't help me much, since Neve Daniel seems to have a weather system all its own...

Sink? What Sink?

I've almost forgotten what it's like to have a bathroom sink. It is nearly two months since our sink fell into the cabinet below it, back in early February. We offered to have the sink fixed before it had finally fallen, and take the cost off of our rent, but the landlady thought the estimate (around 250 shekels) was way too high, and thought that another handyman, Dror, could fix it with silicone for much less. Yesterday, Dror finally arrived. He took a look at the sink and started to laugh. Why was he laughing? Because the landlady told him he could fix it with silicone! Of course, I laughed too. Every time there is a problem in the house, she tells us she will "come fix it with silicone" (and never does). She did not laugh at all when Dror told her that now it would be 450 shekels to fix it. And that didn't even include making the hot water work, or fixing the leaky toilet upstairs. (We couldn't help but laugh when he saw that the toilet could indeed be fixed with silicone. I would let her do it herself, if I actually thought she would come.)

One way or another, it seems that we might actually have a working sink in the near future.

Journal Entry #121: Tuesday, April 1

Interesting Phenomenon

For those who don't know, for Passover we must remove all of our "regular" food from our homes and replace it with specially Kosher for Passover foods. To this end, stores in America that cater to the Jewish crowd start stocking up on these specially Kosher for Passover food items in, like, February. Here in Israel, however, it's two weeks before Passover and I haven't seen a thing in any of the stores except Bamba (more on that later.) None of the lined shelves, cases of matzos, jars of borscht, or anything Manischewitz. What does this tell me? At least one thing: OUR Kosher for Passover food is going to be a lot fresher than THEIR Kosher for Passover food! (Am I tempting anyone? There are still rooms available at the hotels here!)

Oh, About Bamba

First of all, allow me to clarify: Bamba, a peanut butter-corn puff snack-food, is only acceptable on Passover for people of Spanish/Mediterranean descent who eat legumes on Passover. (If you can't recall fond memories of your mother spreading peanut butter on your matzah, chances are you don't fall into this category.)

Secondly, what is so significant about ready-for-Passover Bamba? Well, apparently Bamba is high on the list of requirements for national security. In fact, the government has declared that in a national emergency, such as a missile strike, the Bamba factory workers would be included on the list of those who must go to work. I kid you not! Why is making Bamba so important? Well, this will give you a bit of insight into the priorities of the Israeli people: it's because the children love it so much. Imagine that! After all, what could be more important to a country's security than the security (even emotional security) of its children? (Oh, and I've been seeing Kosher for Passover Bamba since *before* February. Apparently, they're not taking any chances!)

Journal Entry #122: Wednesday, April 2

It's Not Just History

Tonight, Lawrence and I were delighted to accompany our daughter

Lexi to a special party for the girls in their 6th grade class and their parents, in honor of their Bat Mitzvah year. I had no idea what to expect, but I never expected what we got. The girls put on a play that brought me to tears. (And I didn't even understand the words!) They reenacted the story of the roots of Gush Etzion: The joy that the early pioneers had in building the land from scratch, back in the 40s. The anguish when it seemed that all was lost, after the brutal Arab attack in 1948 on Kfar Etzion. The return, in 1967, of the children who had been orphaned nineteen years before, to rebuild what had been so cruelly taken from them. Then the finale: present-day Gush Etzion with girls in costume representing each of the 14 neighborhoods that make up this wonderful place that we live in. How beautiful it was to see 11- and 12-year-old girls identifying with and reenacting the circumstances of Gush Etzion – their home – coming into being.

My daughter and her friends ARE our future

As I watched and let the incredible feelings that the play invoked wash over me, I couldn't help but think: How many American children know, let alone identify with, anything that happened in America over 50 years ago? But then, one cannot really compare. For we are not just living in Israel. We are living the memories of the past, the reality of the present, the promise and hope of the future; We are truly living the land.

Parental Pride

Of course my daughter had a part in the play as well. I don't know who she played or what she said, but when she opened her mouth to speak, mine and Lawrence's dropped open. There was my little American immigrant daughter, standing up there in front of hundreds of people, stringing together all these Hebrew words effortlessly and with an Israeli accent to boot! (To my ears, anyway. I'm sure a native would think otherwise.) We were so proud! (and shocked!) Apparently, so were her teachers. One of them, who has been speaking English to Lexi in class, commented that she didn't realize Lexi could speak Hebrew and for now on she would talk to her in Hebrew only. Hey, I'm her MOTHER and I didn't know she could speak Hebrew.

Self-Disclaimer

By the way, about my not understanding all the Hebrew in the show; it's not that my Hebrew is so bad; they just used these microphones that made them all sound like they had cotton in their mouths. But perhaps I might still have my 11-year-old daughter teach me a thing or two...

Journal Entry #123: Tuesday, April 8

Passover Cleaning (Ugh!)

Alright, so not *everything* has been elevated to the level of bliss after making Aliyah. Cleaning was never my forte. Lucky for me I have all FOUR(!) of my kids home to "help" clean for *Pesach* (Passover), since their vacation starts 1½ weeks before the actual holiday. (Can you imagine American parents putting up with that?) In other words, I not only have to clean, but I have to be a General Manager for an unwilling staff of four. This includes coming up with all sorts of workplace incentives (ice cream is very effective) and outings during break time. After our first work day, I rewarded the girls with a sleepover with friends. The boys created their own reward: their toys were so organized that they could truly find something to play with.

I have actually eliminated three days from the cleaning agenda. We are planning on taking a trip up to the Galilee on Friday and not returning until Sunday night. This is in place of taking a similar trip on Passover. It's less than half the price, and I expect just a fraction of the crowds. Of course that is because everyone else will be doing what I am running away from – Passover cleaning!

Hebrew Is Sneaking Up On Us

My children's progress in learning Hebrew has been very individual. Surprisingly enough, Ezra has been taking the longest. He doesn't really speak, and claims not to understand. So it came as quite a surprise the other day when I told a Hebrew-speaking guest of ours, in Hebrew, what Ezra was about to ask him, and Ezra then told me that he didn't need to ask him since I just did.

A Road Map To Where?

Go, go Coalition forces! Around here, people seem to be strongly in favor of what Bush is doing in Iraq, myself included. Of course, there are a lot of Arabs around here as well and I haven't exactly taken a poll in Bethlehem. However, they haven't been particularly quiet about their wishes that Saddam should blast America, Britain, and Israel off the face of the planet. Isn't it so great that Bush and Blair have this nice plan to first eliminate terror-sponsoring, tyrannically-run Iraq, and then do their "Road Map" by taking a chunk of tiny Israel and turning it into a brand new country of actual terrorists who can't wait to thank Bush for his good deed by blowing up him and his country? Actually, I haven't quite figured out the logic in this...

Journal Entry #124: Wednesday, April 9

Finally, The News You've All Been Waiting For...

Our sink is fixed! Man, is my landlady lucky. I don't know who the guy felt worse for – her or us. Remember that months ago, when the sink was just loosening, we had a guy named Yoav who was going to charge 250 shekels to fix it. Our landlady said "No way," and that she would take care of it.

Many weeks later, after the sink had fallen, of course, she got a quote from her handyman of choice, D'ror, for 450 shekels. We told D'ror to just do it already, that we would just take it off of our rent. When we called to arrange a time, he said that she called him and told him not to come. Furious, I called her to find out what was going on. She told me she was getting it done for cheaper – by YOAV! And you know what? He agreed to fix the whole darn thing for 150 shekels!! We were stunned. And embarrassed to pay him so little. As I wrote the check, after he had done hours of work (and with an employee) I asked him how he had come to that amount. He told me he just felt so bad about the whole thing, and didn't think she would fix it for more. (I challenge you to find me a handyman anywhere else who would have done that...)

Advantage Of A Small House...

...It takes much less time to clean. Yesterday we hired a local teenager to help get "started" on Passover cleaning. In half a day she finished everything except the girls' rooms (the girls had done them already) and the kitchen. Tomorrow she will come help us do the kitchen, and that is it, folks. Only problem is after we make our whole house kosher for Passover, it kind of limits what we can eat in it. We will probably be spending a lot of time at the pizza store.

Journal Entry #125: Thursday, April 10

No More Excuses

Okay, this is it. If you have been thinking about making Aliyah, and you just need that one little push, that "piece d'resistance" to get you to do it; I have got it! Are you ready for this? In Israel you can get kosher, *mehadrin, cholov yisroel* (very, very kosher) Ben & Jerry's ice cream for Passover! That did it, right? Are you packing your bags, or what? Maybe you can still get onto one of the Nefesh B'Nefesh planes this summer. Hey, I bought eight pints! (But maybe I should buy some more...)

Last Big Trip Before D-Day

Of course I mean Delivery Day. As I am approaching the 35-week mark in my pregnancy, we are about to take a big family trip to the Galil and the Golan, for a three-day weekend with a group of families from Efrat. The real purpose of the trip is starting to seem a bit hazy – it was supposed to alleviate the need to prepare for Shabbat in the midst of all the Passover preparation. And, it has done that. However I haven't exactly saved time. Oh well, who cares. The only bummer about the trip for me is that Sunday is skiing day. I am not much into spectator sports – I like to get in on the action. You don't suppose they would rent skis to big, round me, do you? Don't worry; I wouldn't even think of it (well, I would think of it, but I wouldn't do it). Luckily in THIS country you can go up the ski lift without skis, and you can even take a round trip. I guess I'll play photographer this time around.

Visting in the Galil

Journal Entry #126: Sunday, April 13

Our Escape From Passover Cleaning

A highly recommended activity! We started on Friday afternoon with a beautiful drive through the Jordan Valley up to the Lower Galilee. Wow! We had never driven that road before and it was truly delightful. The route started as a descent from the hills of the city of Jerusalem which sit at about 900 meters above sea level. As we headed east through progressively drier and more barren mountains, we went increasingly lower until we were several hundred meters *below* sea level (yes, our ears were popping!) My kids had a lot of difficulty understanding being below "sea level" since we weren't under water and saw nothing that even resembled water. Coming from Florida, they had a good point!

When we reached the Dead Sea we turned north. It was on this two-lane country road that we wound our way from the desert towards the rolling green hills of the Lower Galilee. There is nothing like taking a drive like that, with your whole family, where every member of the family from the moody teenager to the rambunctious kindergartener just "Ooohs" and "Aaaahs" the whole ride. That Lawrence and I would appreciate the scenery was a given. But hearing my children say things like, "Wow, I've never seen anything so beautiful," – now that made the whole trip!

Weather Or Not

Something amazing about Israel is how it seems almost like ten geographically different countries packed into one tiny little place. How can a country so small have such varied topography and with so many different climates? I often talk about how Neve Daniel has its own private weather system. Such is true in many parts of Israel. Our trip this weekend perfectly illustrated this point. Without ever getting on a plane, we experienced "summer" and "winter." Shabbat in the Lower Galilee was at a field school near Mount Tabor (of the Biblical story of Deborah the Prophetess). Everything there was green and lush. There were wildflowers all over. It was quite warm, and there were a few too many uninvited guests in the form of mosquitoes and other flying critters. Summer.

Riding the ski lift

On Sunday, we drove an hour and a half further north, to Mount Hermon in the Golan Heights. We were greeted by beautiful snow-capped mountains and freezing weather. (Okay, so it wasn't 32-degrees freezing, but it was cold enough that I was freezing!) Winter.

The most complicated part of the trip was packing for such drastic fluctuations in temperature and weather!

Change In Plans

As for going to Mount Hermon Ski Area, luckily for me the family decided that sledding would be the activity as opposed to skiing. Not that I could have done either, but we were able to all go up the non-skiers chair-lift together. I held the bags and took pictures (and froze) while the rest of the family sledded. Oh, and about that chair-lift. Did I ever mention that Israelis have a very different safety standard than Americans? What? Only 45 times? Well, here's number 46: ANYONE can go up the darn thing. I tried to read the all-in-Hebrew rules posted at the lower chair-lift terminal. I can't tell you what it said, but nowhere did it say anything about restrictions such as height, age, heart or back trouble, pregnancy, etc. I figured there must be such rules and I must have missed them so I asked if I could ride and they said it was no problem. I'd already seen other children ride so I knew it would be ok to take even my 6-year-old, so we all got on, and I rode with little Ezra.

My Chair Lift Adventure

Have you ever been on a chair lift? They're all somewhat different, but this one was very basic. Two at a time, a single safety bar that lowers in front of you, and it doesn't stop at all when you are getting on or off. Now this may sound somewhat retarded, but I was never particularly good at getting off of chair lifts. I also have this little minor problem of being afraid of heights. When they stuffed me and Ezra into this rapidly-moving chair thing, I discovered that there was basically nothing holding Ezra in at all and we were mighty high off the ground! I basically held onto Ezra for dear life and begged him not to look down (since looking down involves *leaning* down!)

As we rode up the interminably long thing, we passed dozens of passengers making their way down. You can't imagine how many people had children much smaller than my Ezra. What were they thinking?! For that matter, what was I thinking?! Of course all that was the least of my troubles – for at the top I had to get OFF of the lift. Two burly dudes were there to assist people. In fact, I think their paycheck for the day was earned when I arrived. I was in the seat on the left, the rest of my family was waiting for me to the right. I psyched myself up for the big dismount and prepared to grab Ezra and dash to the right. Except that I was wrong. What I found out afterwards (Oh why didn't I watch Eitan and Lexi get off?!?) is that the person on the right is supposed to go to the right, and the person on the left is supposed to go to the left just for a second until the chair passes and then cross over to the right. That is why they purposely had me sit on the left side because they thought I was somewhat intelligent and only intelligent people get to sit on the left side. Boy, did I prove them wrong!! So imagine this: I got off holding Ezra and moved towards the right. The guy on the right also grabbed Ezra and pulled him towards the right. Meanwhile, the guy on the left was pulling me towards the left and barking instructions (as only real Israelis know how) that I could barely hear let alone understand and obey. All this took place in little more than seconds and all I could think was that even in sneakers I just couldn't seem to get off of a chair lift gracefully. Then I looked down at my huge belly and remembered that these days I don't do ANYTHING gracefully, and at least they wouldn't have been expecting me to! (Besides, they let me up on that thing; they just had to face the consequences!)

The Best Part

As we were heading towards our car there was a tractor/snowblower/ plow that went into action in the area of the parking lot. No big deal, I thought, and barely gave it another glance. Until I noticed that everyone else in the parking lot had stopped dead in their tracks and were all watching as if it were the event of the year. Wait – it gets better. People were taking pictures, videos, I mean this tractor got top billing! And I'm talking about grown men, soldiers, EVERYONE! The best part? The tractor didn't accomplish a thing! There was no fresh snow, there was nothing at all to plow. But with such a reaction, I'll bet he goes out and plows and blows snow for "no reason" every single day!

6

Living...

Journal Entry #127: Sunday, April 20

The First (And Only) Seder

For 33 years I have had two Seders on Passover. I must say, that was one habit that was very easy to break!! Seder night is truly special, with so much anticipation and preparation preceding it, that there is something anticlimactic about having a "do over" the next night (as everyone who lives outside of Israel must do). No more of that! Here we can put everything we've got into one special night, and relax when it is over. Not that we had everything at our Seder, but what was missed, need not be permanently absent each year. I am referring to our extended families. Of course it would be great if they chose this time next year to take a trip to Israel and spend Pesach with us, but as non-residents of Israel, they would still have to make a second Seder. What I really hope is that one day soon they will be with us permanently; celebrating one Seder, together, each year.

All Over Israel At Once

That could have been the slogan for the wonderful place we went to today called Mini Israel. Opened this winter, it is a walk-through park with incredible miniatures of many of the special places in Israel. Of course, as the newest attraction in Israel it seems that everyone in the country had the same idea to go there. It didn't matter – it was worth it! It was so packed that shortly after my husband and our friend ran back to the car to put some stuff there, they closed the gates. The guys had to practically beg their way back into the park.

A couple of especially notable mentions at the park: the Knesset building with actual marching toy guards, one of which lowers and raises a miniature Israeli flag; the exhibit of the fortress of Latrun which, when approached from a particular angle, overlooks the actual fortress of Latrun (so cool!);

Touring Israel – mini style

The soccer stadium that has an "actual" game going on with a ball that gets kicked into the goals and fans that do "the wave"; the Hermon ski resort with tiny skiers zigzagging down the mountain, and a miniature working chairlift. Of course the Old City of Jerusalem is replicated in incredible detail, as well as numerous other landmarks, attractions and important buildings and it is all laid out in the form of a Jewish star.

Best Of All? The Place Was Open

Well of course it was, you're saying. But that's only because it was a place in Israel. I know that Passover holiday event-seekers in the States didn't have nearly the choices we had here: Today is a legal holiday in America as it is Easter Sunday. This meant slim-pickings as to what was open for Passover vacation business! Just one more great advantage to living a Jewish life in the Jewish state...

Journal Entry #128: Thursday, April 24

Like Being In A Time Warp

How strange it is that as I write this entry, 24 hours after the end of Passover, my family and friends in America still have another seven or eight hours left of eating *matzah*. For the uninitiated, not only are we seven hours ahead of Eastern Time, but Israel's Passover is over after only seven days, as opposed to the rest of the world's eight. It feels like we jumped ahead a day and a half in a time machine. (And we love it!)

Nothing Like A Bargain

On Tuesday we met friends at an Inflatable Fair. (What else do you call it? You know, bounce houses, climbing things, bungee runs, etc.) Anyway, we only had an hour to spend there and they wanted to charge us 80 NIS per family. Since I was obviously not doing any bouncing, and the other adults claimed they wouldn't either, we asked if we could get in for cheaper. She agreed to 60 NIS per family. Pulling out a 100 shekel bill, my husband offered it to see if she would accept that much for the two families. She accepted it – and gave him 10 shekels change!

Journal Entry #129: Tuesday, April 29

Our UnSinkable Saga Continues

After two months of lying on the floor of our cabinet, you can hardly blame the bathroom sink for springing a few leaks from kinked pipes and stuff. Of course, neither can we tolerate it. We called our landlady's favorite handyman, Yoav, who had just fixed the sink for the ridiculously low price of 150 NIS, to come and evaluate the leak. Our landlady had Yoav explain the diagnosis to her over the phone in detail. Like, what parts would he require? And exactly what was he planning to replace? After he spent all that time on the evaluation and explaining it to her, she proclaimed that SHE was going to fix it. We were mortified! Meanwhile, let's see how long it takes her!

Desert Weather

As wet as our winter has been, we still live in something of a desert. I tasted it on Friday, and I am not being metaphorical. We actually had a dust storm. Something that Florida weather had not prepared me for. Of course I knew exactly what it was without even seeing a weather report. It looked almost like a cloudy, foggy day except the color was wrong. It wasn't grey. More like off-white. When I told Lawrence that I thought we were having a desert dust storm and that I was tasting and breathing it, he thought I was nuts. Until he saw the layer of dust on everything in our house. Later we read the forecast: "Dust storms likely throughout". For once, they were right!

A Special Time To Be In Israel

Today commenced a week of very special days for the Jewish people and for Israel in particular. Today was *Yom HaShoah*, or Holocaust Memorial Day. I know that there were special gatherings and programs throughout the Jewish and non-Jewish world today, but somehow being in Israel, living the ultimate dream of so many of the survivors and the victims, was all the more poignant.

Next Tuesday is *Yom HaZikaron*, or Memorial Day. Unlike Memorial Day in America, which to most people I know is a day off of work to shop at all the sales and have a barbecue; here it is especially important and meaningful. There is hardly anyone in the country who has not been personally touched by the loss of a soldier. To have a "memorial" day about something you have in your own memory is much more significant than a "memorial" day about what you only learned from history books – if you were even paying attention.

Next Wednesday is a very joyous day in Israel as it is *Yom Ha'Atzmaut*, or Independence Day. This is the day that commemorates the birth of the modern Jewish state in 1948. It is marked with many festivities about which I will surely be able to enumerate after next Wednesday since it has been many years since I have experienced it for myself here in Israel. However, one particular event that I know of in advance is the special "flag ceremony" that will be taking place in our own Neve Daniel celebration. I know about it because my 13-year-old Shira will be participating in it along with the rest of the seventh graders in our neighborhood. How incredible it will be to celebrate our first Yom Ha'Atzmaut as Israelis among hundreds of my neighbors watching my own daughter in formation with the other kids as they will be parading the huge Israeli flags while marching to the inspiring music!

Journal Entry #130: Monday, May 5

A Timely Event

Tonight we went to an event in Israel that was actually on time. Exactly on time. At precisely 8:00 p.m. the nationwide siren signaling the beginning of *Yom HaZikaron*, Memorial Day, was heard. It also signaled the beginning of the special memorial ceremony that was held in Neve Daniel, and no doubt dozens, if not many hundreds, of others in communities throughout Israel. I debated going to the ceremony. After all, it was after the boys' bedtime and I didn't even have a car to get me up the steep Neve Daniel hill. (Okay, bedtime was just an excuse – it was the hill.) Luckily a neighbor had space for one in her car. The kids hiked, I rode.

We arrived at the social hall 10 minutes before the starting time. The place was empty. What a shame, I thought, that such an important event is so poorly attended. Was I ever wrong! Somehow, in those 10 minutes, the hall packed to standing-room-only. It was actually most fascinating that at an Israeli event, in Israel, attended by Israelis, everyone in attendance was exactly on time. I'd always thought that to be an oxymoron. I don't think I'd have believed it if I hadn't been there myself.

I had mixed feelings about bringing the boys, because of their ages and not really knowing what to expect. I was told, however, that it was perfectly appropriate for all of my children. I prepared the boys by explaining to them that Yom Hazikaron is a special day to remember all of the soldiers who died protecting Israel. After some age-appropriate questions and answers I felt that they had sufficient understanding and we went to the event. As I mentioned, it started with a siren which was honored by standing and perfect silence in the room. I thought the silence would be the only thing my boys understood. After that the whole thing was conducted in Hebrew. It's amazing how even an atmosphere can be felt. Not understanding a word of the proceedings, Ezra leaned over to me and said, "Mom, I'm starting to be very sad."

The brief ceremony ended on an upbeat note with everyone singing *Hatikvah* ("The Hope"), the national anthem. Every one of my children was glad they attended. Their mother was too.

Journal Entry #131: Tuesday, May 6

And Now, For The Moment We've All Been Waiting For...

...It's a boy!!! Who would have believed that my Aliyah baby, my first Sabra (Israeli-born), would have been born on *Yom Ha'Atzmaut*, Israel's Independence Day? If you are double checking your handy-dandy Jewish calendar, yes, Yom Ha'Atzmaut comes out on May 7th this year, but the Jewish date starts the night before. Our son, having been born at 9:31 p.m., is a bonafide Yom Ha'Atzmaut baby! Of course, right away the name suggestions have been pouring in; names like "Yisroel" (Israel), "Amichai" (My Nation Lives), "Cherut" (Freedom), "Zion" and the like. I guess we have eight days to ponder that one. And if you happen to be in Israel in eight days and would like to be of the first to know, you're welcome to join us at our son's Bris next Wednesday morning in Neve Daniel.

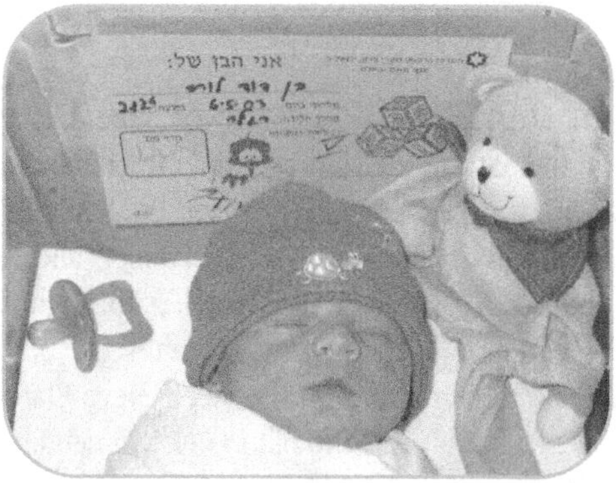

My Aliyah baby

Vital Stats

3.4 kg (about 7 ½ pounds), lots of dark hair, those dark blue eyes that will change one day, and a very cute face. (Not that I'm biased or anything).

His birth was a miracle as all births are, however his was particularly miraculous: the umbilical cord was wrapped around his neck and had a knot in it. Thank G-d, though we were all blissfully unaware of any potential danger, by the time it was discovered the danger had passed and he was born safely.

You Can't Have Everything...

While I was laboring in the hospital towards my ultimate goal, my daughter, Shira, was in Neve Daniel performing in her first Yom Ha'Atzmaut event in the flag ceremony. I had actually contemplated trying to stay in Neve Daniel until after the ceremony, but then I used my brain and asked someone to videotape it instead.

Journal Entry #132: Wednesday, May 7

The Shaarei Tzedek Hospital Experience

Let's just say it's a good thing to be experienced for this experience. Being on my fifth child and being a nurse who is quite familiar with a maternity ward qualifies me as such. You really do need to fend for yourself. Despite having been briefed by various friends on what to expect, I would never have eaten if I hadn't asked around to find out where to find food. The food doesn't come to you; you have to go to it!

Mom and son

Breakfast in the maternity dining room was like a ladies' slumber party. So many women in pajamas having breakfast together and chitchatting like old friends. I couldn't help but wonder if they actually all knew each other or perhaps they recognized each other from the last time they had babies. Since they all seemed to know exactly what to do, I'd say that was a very real possibility...

One great advantage to an Orthodox Jew delivering in an Orthodox Jewish hospital is actually being able to eat the food. Though the meals here aren't reputed to be that good (for good reason, I can now attest) you can go to one of the many kiosks or even to the hospital cafeteria to supplement your meals with just about anything. Which brings me to the only disadvantage to having your baby on Yom Ha'Atzmaut: everything is closed!

The Bottom Line

You know what is so amazing? Despite the fact that this was my most difficult labor; That one must really fend for oneself here; that the towels they give you are the size of postage stamps; That the food leaves much to be desired; that there is no juice to be found anywhere in the whole hospital and that I need to manually crank up the head of my bed, I can honestly say that this was my most incredible birth experience.

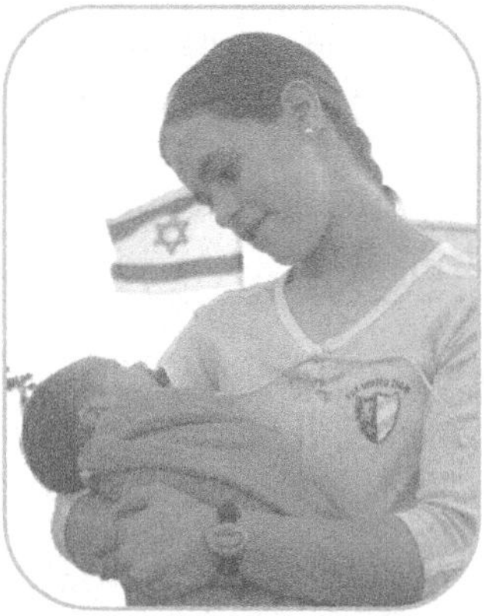

Sister and new brother

Maybe it's because of the miracles of my son's birth; Possibly it has to do with the incredible date that became my son's birthday and how much meaning this special day already had to us this year; Perhaps it is merely the fact that I can sit on my bed, holding and breathing in the scent of my new baby as I gaze out of my huge window overlooking Jerusalem. I suppose it is all of these things, and so much more.

Our new life in Israel is so different than ever before because of the value we have learned to place on what really has meaning. Who cares how big a towel is? I can always take two. How can having a plush towel compete with having a baby in the land of Israel, in Jerusalem, the holiest city in the world? I rest my case.

Journal Entry #133: Tuesday, May 13

Whirlwind Week

Don't tell my kids, but I was very happy that they decided to keep me in the hospital until Friday morning (one extra night). Despite having several adults around to help, it's been non-stop action since I got home!

In anticipation of the *Shalom Zachor* (special Friday night party to welcome a newborn son) all of the neighbors demonstrated their handiness in the kitchen by producing a beautiful (and massive) array of cakes and pastries. (We froze the leftovers. We may still have some when we make the baby's bar-mitzvah).

Shortly before Shabbos I was shocked when my Aunt Wittie from Vermont walked into my house, having snuck away from a Switzerland vacation to be with me at this time. Of course my mom is here as well.

The Shalom Zachor was very special, with friends and neighbors all coming and going after Friday night dinner. I was sound asleep before clean-up even started, but magically it was all completed when I woke up.

Just For Kids

This evening we did something very special. There is a tradition on the night before a baby's bris, children gather around the baby's crib to say special prayers over the baby to ward off anything that may interfere with the bris. We had not done this for our other boys, but thought it was a beautiful thing and decided to do it.

Shema Yisrael

We invited all of the little children we know. (Close to 20 came!) We brought the baby outside since the weather was perfect. All the children gathered around our son. As we all stood there under the Neve Daniel sky, our magnificent view bright and visible in the late afternoon sun, the children said the *Shema* (special prayer) over our new baby. Then everyone joined in singing *Hamalach Hagoel* ("The Angel who Redeems"). It was a beautiful event.

Journal Entry #134: Wednesday, May 14

The Bris

What an unbelievable event! It took place in the social hall in Neve Daniel. Our good friend catered it (our very first catered affair after 15 years of marriage) and the room was set up magnificently. Around seventy-five guests attended coming from Gush Etzion, Jerusalem, and some from much further. Our

The joy of a new father

My Father, the Sandek

gem of a pediatrician was the *mohel*. My father, who is in Neve Daniel for the first time, was the *sandek* (Godfather).

I stood up there watching, surrounded by friends and family, and was overwhelmed by the extraordinary event that was taking place. Here we were, in Israel, our home; with our new son, a "sabra" born on Yom Ha'Atzmaut (Independence Day); joining him to our nation with a covenant that has united our people for 3500 years. My eyes welled up with tears as my father, honored with the naming of the baby, pronounced his name: *Yaakov Zecharia.*

The Naming

Having used the remaining three grandfathers' names up on Ezra, we had to do some serious thinking to come up with a name for this new baby. After much thought without any serious contenders at the forefront Lawrence came up with the names Yaakov and Zecharia. He suggested them to me and I surprised him by not saying "no way".

Actually I liked the names very much. One day I decided to look up Zecharia in the Torah to see what he was all about since I had never learned about him. I did not find out much since the account didn't exactly read like a simple story. My frustration was short-lived. That *very night* I went to a pre-Purim class. Who did I learn about? Not Mordechai and Esther, but Zecharia! The very same day that I wanted to learn about Zecharia because I had *never learned about him before in my whole LIFE!*

Of course as I've mentioned, as soon as the baby was born on Yom Ha'Atzmaut, the name suggestions came pouring in; "Thanks for the suggestion," we would politely say each time, though we had decided on "Yaakov Zecharia" before he was born.

Truth be told, we already had the "Yom Ha'Atzmaut" theme in mind. Despite the fact that I had *every intention* of having the baby on Yom Ha'Atzmaut, we certainly didn't *expect* it. It would not have changed our line of thinking in any case. We made Aliyah just this past year. We appreciate

The Ben-Davids

every day that we are Jews living in a free Jewish state in the land that was promised to us so many years ago. Perhaps other Israelis appreciate it every day as I hope we always will. But in our minds, we didn't need to have the baby on Yom Ha'Atzmaut to make us feel any more connected to this land or this country. The fact that he was born on that day was simply icing on the cake. (And a great ending to a book!)

So Why Yaakov Zecharia?

Our forefather *Yaakov* (Jacob in the Bible) came to Israel on "Aliyah" after his forced exile to his Uncle Lavan's house. (And, I may point out, when he returned he came back via "*derech Beit Lechem*" – Bethlehem – which is right here!)

Living in Gush Etzion, right along "Derech Avot", (Path of the Patriarchs) and not far from *Me'arat Hamachpeilah*, where our forefathers are buried, we feel a strong connection to them and felt inclined to reflect that in the naming of our son. We narrowed it down in by noting that Abraham and Isaac are the fathers to other nations, but Yaakov is the father solely of *Bnai Yisroel* (The Children of Israel. And "Israel" is the other name given to Yaakov). To all of those people who have been telling us to name our baby "Yisroel", we did! We just used his other name.

Zecharia the Prophet was one of the relatively small number of Jews who *made Aliyah* (returned to Israel) from the Babylonian exile. He made Aliyah when it wasn't very popular at all. It was time for the Jews to return but the people did not take advantage.

Zecharia merited seeing the second Temple be built. He also hid many of the vessels of the Temple and other treasures to protect them from foreign kings, and they remain hidden to this day. We hope that giving the name "Zecharia" to our son will be a blessing to our meriting to see those treasures found and put into use in the third Temple.

My son Ezra asked at one point, many months ago, what we would name the baby. We told him we would think of a name. He said, "You don't have to think of a name, *HaShem* (G-d) puts the name in your mind!"

Interestingly enough, a few months ago we asked each one of our children separately for their own suggestions of a name. Would you believe that every one of our children *independently* came up with the name "Yaakov"? I guess it was our children who were the ones worthy of G-d "putting the name in their minds", because who has ever heard of four different people coming up with the same name independently, and with no prompting or common reasons?

Yaakov

Epilogue

All good things must come to an end. On this incredible high, I am concluding this journal to prepare it as the book you are now reading. However, after writing the journal entry about Yaakov's bris, I felt that a certain cycle had been completed and it would be a fitting ending to the journal. I said as much to the readers of my e-journal and was astonished when a flood of e-mails came begging me not to stop.

Then life happened. Life had to be reported on. Thus was begun "Journal II" which continues on to this day; the frequency of its entries depends on the incidence of interesting incidents.

One entry in particular garnered a place in this book, despite its much later date of occurrence. This entry received widespread circulation and only the announcement of Yaakov's birth produced more responses than this one. I therefore present to you:

Journal II Entry #45: December 30

The Kotel

How embarrassing that my baby, a Sabra, has been living his whole life (nearly 8 months) a mere 25 minutes from the *Kotel* (The Western Wall), the holiest site on this earth – and I've never taken him there!!! Jews all over the world pray three times a day towards this spot, and I couldn't take an afternoon and bring him there? (Well, you see, the parking is terrible there, and there are all these stairs, and the stroller...okay, I'll stop.)

Today was the perfect opportunity. I was in Jerusalem, Yaakov was with me, I didn't have a car to deal with parking, and I had TIME – a precious commodity – after an expected eternity at the Ministry of Health turned into six minutes. So we hopped into a cab and were driven way closer than I ever could have parked. Eitan, now 9, and Ezra, 7, marched off to the men's side. They wanted to bring Yaakov since he is a (very) little man, but I had waited 7 ½ months for this – it was my moment!

The Kotel plaza was rather crowded today, but the moment my sons walked off, the rest of the people melted away. It was just me and my Yaakov as I softly explained to him where we were and why this place is so special to us. I brought him right up to the wall and patiently waited for an opening in the sea of praying women. When it came, I placed Yaakov's little hand on the stones and savored that special moment. Then I slowly backed away, Yaakov staring silently ahead, as if he, too, felt the extraordinary feelings that were washing over me.

I know Yaakov won't remember today. We don't even have any pictures to prove he was there. But if it is important to speak to a baby, to play with him, let him hear music, see colors, have experiences, then what more meaningful experience is there to have, than to go to the most spiritual place in the world?

A view of the Old City

Patrons

In honor of
the matriarch of our family

Rena Fishman עמו"ש

Who has always and continues to teach us
grace and generosity and is so proud
of her grandchildren and great-grandchildren.

In memory of our cherished, departed parents

Edward Fishman ע"ה
George Ginsberg ע"ה
Esther Ginsberg ע"ה

Who are looking down from their heavenly abode
with such pride and nachas.

Dedicated to our dear daughter

Laura עמו"ש

Whose life is committed to our ideals,
living our dream and
perpetuating all that we hold dear.

Marty & Carol Ginsberg

In honor of my grandchildren
and great grandchildren

Grandma Rena

To our dear sister Laura

In your Aliyah,
you carried with you
not only the hopes,
dreams and aspirations
of 2,000 years of Jewish history,
but our hopes and dreams as well.
You have had the courage to do
that which we all dream of.
Thanks for taking us
(and the rest of the world)
along for the ride.

May we, and all your readership follow your lead.

Steven and Deena
Yisroel and Amy
Tully and Hindy
Adam and Hudi

(And all the nieces and nephews)

To our niece

Laura

With love and pride
Aunt Dinah & Uncle Marvin
Steve & Maggie
Brian & Josi
Debbie & Rob
as well as Eliana, Jacob, Julia, Michaela,
Simon and Micah

In loving memory of my ...

Husband

Irwin Diamond

Parents

Louis and Sarah Ziffer

Brother

Joseph Ziffer

Sister and Brother-in-law

Beatrice and Benjamin Karp

Brother-in-law

Seymour Diamond

Son-in-law

Arthur DeFrancis

They are forever in my heart.
Pearl Diamond

In honor of

Pearl and Irwin Diamond

With Love
From Their Adoring Family

Dennis and Elizabeth
Matthew and Rae
Cori and Steve
Sarah, Jacqueline, Liana, Gabe, and Alexander

In honor of our parents
Rose and Philip Ziffer

and

In memory of our parents
Irene and Leo Simon

Flo and Larry Ziffer

In honor of our grandchildren

Deborah Ariel and Michael Yair Riskin

from Grandma and Zeidie

Our parents' enduring love for ארץ ישראל
inspires us, their grandchildren,
and great-grandchildren every day

In Honor of

Julius Liebb
and
Betty Kurzmann

In Memory of

Samuel Kurzmann ע"ה
and
Rose Liebb ע"ה

With love, respect and admiration,

Moishe and Shaindy Kurzmann
Monsey, New York

In honor of our dear grandchildren

Gabrielle, Meira, Yoni, Ethan
Eitan, Caleb, and Ari

With much love,
Saba and Savta

In memory Of

Moshe and Shaindel Hilsenrath
Markus and Sabine Pfeffer

Erna and Fred Pfeffer

In loving memory of

Margherita Rinaldi

Mario, Dolores, Salvatore,
Maria and Franco Rinaldi

בס"ד

כרך זה מוקדש של אבינו היקר ר' ברוך בענדיט ב"ר מאיר ז"ל נפטר ט' סיון תשל"ז

נולד בעיר מארגאדעטן ולמד בישיבה הרמה בעיר טאשנאד, שם ינק אהבת תורה ויראת שמים, שנשארו עמו כל ימי חייו. כל תשוקות וחמדת חייו היו מרוכזים במשימה אחת: לנטוע בבניו את המשירות ואתת המרץ לתורת ה'. לעולם לא ימוש מזכרוננו את תמונת אבינו ז"ל יושב עם גמרתו בוקר בוקר, משנן ולומד את הדף היומי למשך שנים רבות וארוכות, עד שזכה לסיים את הש"ס כולו כמה פעמים, פזר נתן לאביונים בסתר ובהצנע לכת, ותמך במשפחתו ובלומדי תורה בכסף מלא ולב רחב. מורשתו לא תמוש ממנו לעולם, ונזכה ללכת בעקבותיו כפי מה שלימד אותנו בכל יום ובכל שעה.

ולזכורה של אמנו היקרה ברכה בת ר' משה יצחק ע"ה נפטרה ה' שבת תשס"ה עשרים ושמונה שנה חיתה לאחר פטירת בעלה האהוב והמסור, אבל זכרו וצורתו מעולם לא סרו ממנה. הקימה את משפחתה בכוח ובמרץ, באומץ ובתבונה, באהבה ובחסד, וחפץ ה' בידה הצליח. לעולם נזכור אותה בתוך סמל ומופת לאם יהודיה ולאשת-חיל אמתית ונכונה, אשר הצלחת המשפחה היתה בראש ענייניה ומשאת נפשה.

Made in the USA
Las Vegas, NV
10 August 2021

27878561R00116